THE PASSIONATE & LEADERS SERIES

James R. Lucas & Phil Hotsenpiller

THE PARADOX PRINCIPLE:
HOW PASSIONATE LEADERS MERGE
COMPETING IDEAS

Quintessential Books

READ BOLDLY. THINK DEEPLY. LIVE PASSIONATELY.
www.quintessentialbooks.com
BOSTON • KANSAS CITY

Copyright © 2009, Quintessential Books.

This Book Is Copyrighted Material. All Rights Are Reserved. It Is Against The Law To Make Copies Of This Material Without Getting Specific Written Permission In Advance From Quintessential Books. No Part Of This Publication May Be Reproduced, Stored In A Retrieval System, Or Transmitted In Any Form Or By Any Means, Electronic, Mechanical, Photocopying, Recording, Or Otherwise, Without Prior Written Permission Of The Publisher.

International Rights And Foreign Translation Rights Are Available Only Through Negotiation With Quintessential Books.

Printed In The United States Of America
ISBN 978-0-9823161-3-9

Cover & Layout Design by Barberhaus Design Studios
Cover Design by Jonas Barber
Layout Design by JV Kennedy

Author Photo Of James R. Lucas Copyright © 2006
By Decloud Studio. All Rights Are Reserved. Used By Permission.

Author Photo Of Phil Hotsenpiller Copyright © 2008
By Barry Morgenstein Studios. All Rights Are Reserved. Used By Permission.

READ BOLDLY. THINK DEEPLY. LIVE PASSIONATELY.

Visit Quintessential Books At www.quintessentialbooks.com
For More About Passionate Lives And Leaders, Visit www.livesandleaders.com

All Trademarked Terms Are The Property Of Luman International, Inc. All Rights Are Reserved.

TABLE OF CONTENTS

Introduction: The Surprising Power of Paradox... 6

Part 1: Living Your Life – 5 Paradoxes... 12
    Be an Optimist and *a Realist*..*13*
    Be a Movie Star and *a Stage Hand*..*19*
    Learn from History and *Live in the Moment*..*25*
    Be a Leonardo and *a Washington*..*30*
    Be a Carnegie and *a Scrooge*..*37*

Part 2: Relating to Others – 5 Paradoxes 42
    Move Forward Boldly and *Stop for Correction*..*43*
    Get All Wrapped Up and *Disentangle*..*47*
    Expect Perfection and *Expect Mistakes*..*52*
    Give People the Maximum and *Commute Their Sentences*..*56*
    Be an Iron Fist and *a Velvet Glove*..*62*

Part 3: Producing Better Performance – 5 Paradoxes 68
    Be a Rock and *a Stream*..*69*
    Eliminate Distractions and *Listen for Input*..*74*
    Throw the Dice and *Use the Safe*..*81*
    Be a Racehorse and *a Plow Horse*..*85*
    Push Hard and *Cut Way Back*..*89*

Part 4: When "Either" *Is* the Right Answer 96

Part 5: Merging Competing Ideas – Clearing the Obstacles 100
    Rate Your Organization 103

Time for Action.. 106

THE SURPRISING POWER OF PARADOX

Competing ideas are everywhere. Even the smart people on your team hold passionate differences of opinion. As a leader, you can merge those competing ideas to generate value and produce commitment and passion.

If you're like most people, you lean toward one side or the other of these paradoxes: maybe you're really good at facing the facts but not so good at being optimistic, or perhaps you're a very positive person who doesn't like staring reality in the face.

Passion is squandered when we manage competing ideas poorly, when we embrace one side without the other. But if we can live in the vibrant middle between competing ideas, our organization's passion will increase dramatically and our team's firepower will be unleashed.

Start here, with these 15 personal paradoxes. Spend some time on each one. Don't rush through them. We've prompted you with some provocative questions, but we haven't left you with a lot of room to get your thoughts down. The reason? We want you to try to focus your thoughts and keep them concise - the best course for effective action.

"IF WE CAN LIVE IN THE VIBRANT MIDDLE BETWEEN COMPETING IDEAS, OUR ORGANIZATION'S PASSION WILL INCREASE DRAMATICALLY AND OUR TEAM'S FIREPOWER WILL BE UNLEASHED."

THE PARADOX PRINCIPLE

A paradox is an apparent contradiction.

It looks, to all the world, like its two sides are in conflict. How could you possibly expect perfection *and* expect mistakes at the same time, or move ahead boldly *while* stopping for correction? We often perceive a conflict between the two sides of a paradox, so we tend to choose one or the other. They're mutually exclusive, so we *have* to pick one. Right?

It sounds so logical. Here's an example: A contractor's going to do a repair or remodeling project in your home. You push him on the price, but you also want him to do it quickly. He gets frustrated and hits you with a choice: "Okay, do you want it done cheap or do you want it done fast?"

And you start thinking about which option you want, instead of asking your own question: "Why not *both*? Why can't I have a cheap price *and* a fast schedule?"

Why not indeed.

It's when you answer one of these supposedly "either-or" questions with a strong "both!" answer that you move yourself into a new world of possibilities.

The Japanese automobile industry famously said "both," and it produced higher-quality cars at lower prices than anyone had done before. In fact, pushing for both quality and value at the same time produced astonishing results. As manufacturers took unnecessary steps out of the process, for example, they lowered the cost but also had fewer things to go wrong – so they improved the quality as well.

That's the key. Paradoxes are only *apparent* contradictions. What you see is not what you get – if you will see the paradox in its wholeness.

> **"ONLY THE PARADOX COMES ANYWHERE NEAR TO COMPREHENDING THE FULLNESS OF LIFE."**
> **CARL JUNG, PSYCHOLOGIST[1]**

The Alternative: A Simplistic, Paradox-free World

Let's face it: It's a lot easier to live in a world where you can pick one out of two, where you can focus on the one and ignore the other.

Some leaders fashion themselves as "tough-minded": they move full speed ahead and damn the torpedoes, keep their people at arm's length, prosecute mistakes, nail people who fail to the wall, and are always willing to give people a piece of their mind. They don't have to think; they just have to be tough. The answer is always "my way or the highway."

Other leaders consider themselves to be "collaborative": they always get opinions and are open to correction, consider every team member a family member, are tolerant of human error, give lots of second chances, and are consistently encouraging and supportive. They don't have to think, they just have to be "collaborative." The answer is always "our way is the best way."

These approaches are simplistic. They leave out big chunks of leadership excellence. They miss terrific opportunities to explore the power of "both." They squelch passion or results – or both. They hurt us with the lie that life is an either/or proposition.

The world isn't actually free of paradoxes. But we can put blinders on and be free from thinking about them. Since most people try to live in a paradox-

> **"I WOULD OFTEN ASK [NELSON] MANDELA QUESTIONS LIKE THIS ONE: WHEN YOU DECIDED TO SUSPEND THE ARMED STRUGGLE, WAS IT BECAUSE YOU REALIZED YOU DID NOT HAVE THE STRENGTH...OR BECAUSE YOU KNOW YOU COULD WIN OVER INTERNATIONAL OPINION BY CHOOSING NONVIOLENCE? HE WOULD THEN GIVE ME A CURIOUS GLANCE AND SAY, 'WHY NOT BOTH?'.... THE MESSAGE WAS CLEAR: LIFE IS NEVER EITHER/OR. DECISIONS ARE ALWAYS COMPLEX, AND THERE ARE ALWAYS COMPETING FACTORS. TO LOOK FOR SIMPLE EXPLANATIONS IS THE BIAS OF THE HUMAN BRAIN, BUT IT DOESN'T CORRESPOND TO REALITY."**
>
> **RICHARD STENGEL, TIME MAGAZINE[2]**

free world (a world that doesn't actually exist, except in their heads), we can be comfortable and competitive if we try to live the same way.

But just think of the possibilities if we passionately choose "both!"

Unleashing Passion by Choosing "Both" Over "Either"

Passionate leaders, once they discover the existence and power of paradoxes, make them part of their leadership toolbox.*

They start seeing paradoxes everywhere. Their starting position is "both" and only slowly do they move to "either/or."

"Why not both?" is the answer to a whole host of questions.

For example:
- *Should we keep plowing away toward the deadline, or should we let them know we might have difficulty making it?*
- *Should we keep the heat on the team, or should we give them a break?*
- *Do people on that mega-project need an audacious goal or a safety net?*
- *Should we cut spending in a down market or should we increase spending to take advantage of the down market?*
- *Should we expect people to follow the policies and procedures or to challenge them?*

The answer to all of these is "Yes!" The fun – and the source of passion – lies in working out what that "yes" means.

Passionate leaders are passionate about *all* of life, not just half of it. They know that half a truth is not only incomplete, but in a very real way is a lie.

Seeing the array of paradoxes that make up so much of passionate leadership is the start. Living in the vibrant center of those paradoxes is the middle phase. And building a team that is passionate about the power of "both" – and delivers outsized results – is the happy conclusion.

> **"PARADOXES.... LEADERSHIP IS LOADED WITH THEM."**
> JACK WELCH, FORMER CEO,
> THE GENERAL ELECTRIC COMPANY[3]

---

* *If this idea of paradox resonates with you and you want the outstanding value that can be gained from managing paradoxes, you might also see my book* Broaden the Vision and Narrow the Focus: Managing in a World of Paradox, *which covers 20 organizational paradoxes to complement these personal leadership paradoxes.*

Achieving More by Passionately Mastering 15 Personal Paradoxes

And so here we are, ready to move into the world in which you already live: the world of paradoxes.

We hope this will be an exciting journey for you. We know that your passion for leadership will grow as you explore these 15 personal paradoxes.

Take your time. You could live inside this little book for a few weeks. Some paradoxes will take a little more thought than others. It's okay to spend a few days – or more – considering ways to implement a single paradox.

We've given you some action items for each of these, so you can really master them and make them your own. If you do, you'll be in a very small group, one with an immense competitive advantage.

Should you work hard on this or enjoy it thoroughly?

You know the answer.

"PASSIONATE PEOPLE ARE MOTIVATED TO RECOGNIZE THAT THERE ARE MANY IDEAS THAT OTHERS CAN OFFER. THE GREATEST VALUE IS PROVIDED BY TAKING THE BEST IDEAS AND COMBINING THEM."

DAM AMSDEN, PRESIDENT, AUTOMATION ALLIANCE GROUP

"I THINK YOU BEST MERGE IDEAS BY ALLOWING EVERYONE TO FEEL INFLUENCE ON THE OUTCOME. NOT EVERYBODY GETS THEIR OWN WAY ALL THE TIME, BUT THE IDEAS ARE MERGED IN A TRUE CONSENSUS. IT'S TRULY A COMBINATION OF IDEAS, NOT ONE WINNING OVER THE OTHER. IN THE BEST MERGERS OF IDEAS, PEOPLE WALK AWAY AND SAY, 'YOU KNOW WHAT? I HAD INFLUENCE.'"

JIM FALETTI, PRESIDENT & CEO, HR INSIGHTS, LTD.

LIVING YOUR LIFE – 5 PARADOXES

Since this book concerns personal paradoxes of leadership, we think you'll find many applications for other areas of your life – relationships, parenting, volunteer work, your understanding of politics (for example: "Should we have a strong military or a peaceful diplomacy with everyone?"). You can see how far this paradox business can take you.

Ready to go? Together, let's take ownership of these important life paradoxes.

PARADOX 1: BE AN OPTIMIST AND A REALIST

FIVE PARADOXES FOR LIVING YOUR LIFE
> BE AN OPTIMIST AND A REALIST
  Be a Movie Star and a Stage Hand
  Learn from History and Live in the Moment
  Be a Leonardo and a Washington
  Be a Carnegie and a Scrooge

"HOW WONDERFUL THAT WE HAVE MET WITH PARADOX. NOW WE HAVE SOME HOPE OF MAKING PROGRESS." NIELS BOHR, THEORETICAL PHYCISIST[4]

Be an Optimist

The vast majority of "news" stories report *bad* news. There is a lot wrong with this. It's discouraging and depressing. It makes you disgusted with the human condition. And the worst of it is that this isn't even *accurate*; most of what happens – the everyday stuff of life and a high percentage of the events – is actually just fine.

Optimists live longer, and enjoy that extra time lots more than their dead, pessimistic friends. They have better health. They're more pleasant to be around. They make collaboration less painful and success more likely. They go farther, and they get a lot more out of the ride.

If you're going to be an optimist, there are some things you're going to have to avoid. You have to resist being a news junkie: poison in, pessimism out. What are some other things you could avoid to be more of an optimist?

1. _____

2. _____

3. _____

You can help yourself nurture optimism as well. When facing a big challenge, you could ask yourself first, "What could possibly go *right* with this?" Other actions you could take:

1. _____
2. _____
3. _____

If you get what you expect (and that principle works in a good part of life), you'll get much more worth keeping if you expect the best.

"AN OPTIMIST IS A BASSOONIST WITH A PAGER."[5]

Be a Realist

Without realists, the world would seem a lot less miserable – but only for a little while, until the bad stuff they talk about hit us with full force.

Realists take precautions. They know life can be tough, so they're not surprised when things go south. They're able to keep their balance in the face of trials and tribulations. They keep fellow workers and projects and strategies honest. They don't believe press releases, theirs or yours or anyone else's, which is good for producing the humility that leads to greater success.

But to be an effective realist, you have to stay away from seeing the bad and ugly and disastrous in every situation. You have to teach yourself when to say "stop!" or "enough!" What else can you do to be heard?

1. _____
2. _____
3. _____

You're also going to need to make your realism palatable, by conveying it without exaggeration, fear-mongering, or sarcasm. You could make it go down easier by:

1. _____
2. _____
3. _____

It's easy to spend your life disillusioned by facts and acting on bad information. If you want to make good decisions, be a realist.

"THERE ARE SOME PEOPLE WHO LIVE IN A DREAM WORLD, AND THERE ARE SOME WHO FACE REALITY; AND THEN THERE ARE THOSE WHO TURN ONE INTO THE OTHER." DOUGLAS H. EVERETT[6]

Be a Cut-to-the-Chase Idealist

Living a full, rich life is a lot more likely if we become *realistic optimists*.

You start with the truth — about yourself, your relationships, your work, your dreams. Here's where you are, no fluff or glaze. It is what it is. You face the truth, no matter how ugly. And you get it sorted out and clearly defined and understood. Asking for honest input from a friend or colleague or professional is spot on.

But you don't face the truth so you'll be depressed or killed by it. You face it so you can *improve* it, *build* on it, *change* it. You say, "It is what it is," so you can make it what you want it to be. You want to be an optimist, but one standing on solid rock, not shifting sand. Passionate people are naturally more optimistic, but seriously passionate people won't let their passion be stolen by illusion.

You always want to temper your optimism with a strong dose of reality. And you want to look at reality not through rose-colored glasses but with confidence that no matter what the reality is, something better can be made out of it.

TAKE FRESH ACTIONS TO LIVE THIS PARADOX

Describe a realist you know. What do you like about his or her realism that you could adopt?

_____

_____

_____

Describe an optimist you know. What do you like about his or her optimism that you could adopt?

_____

_____

_____

To be successful, you have to look at things honestly, and you have to look at them hopefully. Pick a situation in your life. What would you have to change in your thinking or actions in order to look at it honestly and hopefully – in equal amounts?

_____

_____

_____

To be happy, you have to find a way to see the bright side and enjoy your life even if the facts are unpleasant. Think of a situation that seemed ugly. What could have changed – something you had control over – to salvage something good out of it?

_____

_____

_____

We've all been encouraged to "take the blinders off" and to "look on the bright side."

Now you know an important truth: you can do both. You can be an idealist – as long as you're a pragmatic one.

Believing in an Industry that Makes Dreams Reality

When Jantiene Berg was 10 years old, she watched Hotel *on television whenever it aired.*

"I tried to imagine what it would be like to be a part of this magical world, to create a backdrop where people forgot about their troubles and where dreams became reality," she remembers. She decided that one day she would be responsible for a hotel like that.

But growing up with a family that owned two businesses, Berg herself was confronted with reality: if you want something you have to work for it. You have to chase that dream and create your own opportunities.

By the age of 14, she started to work in her parents' business and in the kitchens of small restaurants, washing dishes. By 17, she was working in the trendiest restaurant in her home town. She believes that her enthusiasm and curiosity to talk to guests made her successful in her job.

After earning a BA in Economics in the Hotel Management School, Berg started her first job as a sales representative at one of the oldest hotels in Amsterdam: the Victoria Hotel. After three years of hard work and learning about sales and marketing, she moved to The Hague.

She was 25 years old and had her first management job in a city she did not know. "The moment I stepped into the Carlton Ambassador," she reveals, "I felt I belonged in the hotel. I started to explore the city. I did all the important sightseeing and visited my competitors. Before I knew it, I was a member of many societies and was invited to important events." The hotel was growing in name recognition and revenue, and she knew she had played a part in that. "Just before I left, I told a colleague that I would be a general manger by the age of 30 at a hotel like the Carlton Ambassador. If I made it, he told me, he would buy me dinner in a world-class restaurant," Berg says.

She moved to a different company, but after a few months, she knew it was a mistake. This was the first time in her life that she had made a career move for money, and she was surrounded by people who did not work with a passionate drive but instead worked for money. Fighting every day with other egos drained her completely, and the credit for the success she created went to the commercial director. "Everything was beautifully decorated," Berg explains. "Everything and everybody was beautiful, but the environment was not inspiring."

Just when Berg was making plans for a sabbatical, her former employer joined her for coffee. She told him the truth: "I would love to move to another job because I cannot develop myself any more in this company." Before she knew it, he offered her a challenge: to become a general manager of a four-star hotel in Amsterdam.

Her first impression was, "What a beautiful building!" Her second thought was, "This is going to be a job!" The next day, she phoned the managing director to say that she would take the position.

"IF YOU WILL CALL YOUR TROUBLES EXPERIENCES, AND REMEMBER THAT EVERY EXPERIENCE DEVELOPS SOME LATENT FORCE WITHIN YOU, YOU WILL GROW VIGOROUS AND HAPPY, HOWEVER ADVERSE YOUR CIRCUMSTANCES MAY SEEM TO BE."

JOHN HEYWOOD, ENGLISH PLAYWRIGHT AND POET[7]

Berg had to learn everything about the building—what the current guests liked or were missing, what the trends in hospitality were, what could be done to make the hotel different from other hotels in Amsterdam.

It was a childhood dream and longstanding goal transformed into reality.

"I was so proud: I was 30." Berg laughs: *"And dinner was lovely,"* she adds, recalling how her friend made good on his word.

PARADOX 2: BE A MOVIE STAR AND A STAGEHAND

FIVE PARADOXES FOR LIVING YOUR LIFE
Be an Optimist and a Realist
> **BE A MOVIE STAR AND A STAGE HAND**
Learn from History and Live in the Moment
Be a Leonardo and a Washington
Be a Carnegie and a Scrooge

Be a Movie Star

There are times when you just can't help it. You have to be out in front.

Introvert or extrovert, shy or bold, quiet or boisterous – it doesn't matter. The work calls for a star, and you're it. It might just be for that "15 minutes of fame," but for the quarter of an hour you need to exercise the leadership that you alone can offer.

You speak up to challenge an idea in a meeting. You present an alternative that you've been working on in private for weeks. You volunteer to do something that you don't have time to do because you're the best person to make it happen. You question the organization's strategy or goals. They say that being a movie star depends on chance, but usually that kind of chance meets up with a prepared person with just a bit of courage.

Your time on stage will be tough if you don't guard against arrogance. Given who you are, what else should you watch out for when trying to take the lead?

1. _____
2. _____
3. _____

To prepare for an "onstage" moment, you could prepare your comments in advance and review them with a trusted colleague. Think of something coming up on your radar screen. Anything else you could do to exploit the moment?

1. _____

2. _____

3. _____

Most organizations have a few stars, mostly clustering around the top. Great organizations want a lot of stars, want *everyone* to be a star – want *you* to be a star.

"EVEN IF STRENGTH FAIL, BOLDNESS AT LEAST WILL DESERVE PRAISE: IN GREAT ENDEAVORS EVEN TO HAVE HAD THE WILL IS ENOUGH."

PROPERTIUS, ROMAN POET

Be a Stagehand

Even if they don't mean it, movie stars will often give thanks to the "behind-the-scenes" people who made their movies successful. If they're really impressed with themselves, they'll thank all of the "little people" who produced such big results (as if the movie crew had been staffed by leprechauns).

Nothing happens without the stagehands. Their work is supportive and unseen, but that doesn't make it unimportant. No matter what you do, you're either doing something that adds value, or you can make a fuss until they let you do it. No sane leader wants to employ people who aren't making a difference. And no self-respecting person just wants to fill up space.

So being a terrific stagehand involves avoiding busy work and making your time and yourself count. Even if you're the star with top billing, what else can you do (or stop doing) to make a practical difference in your situation right now?

1. _____
2. _____
3. _____

You could take time today to go out of your way to thank one or more of the stagehands in your life. Be specific, and focus on what really adds value. Anything else you can do to encourage excellent stagehand work?

1. _____
2. _____
3. _____

Who counts for more, the movie star or the stagehand? Both, absolutely! Being a valuable stagehand has many intrinsic rewards, and in the long run those outside rewards will come – perhaps even the chance to be the star, like a former stagehand named Harrison Ford.

"A LEADER IS NOT AN ADMINISTRATOR WHO LOVES TO RUN OTHERS, BUT SOMEONE WHO CARRIES WATER FOR HIS PEOPLE SO THAT THEY CAN GET ON WITH THEIR JOBS." ROBERT TOWNSEND, AUTHOR[9]

Be a Hardworking Celebrity

You'll go a lot further in life if you're a *behind-the-scenes star.*

You start with hard work, wherever you are. You're willing to make the copies, run the machine, and handle the ticked-off customer. You're ready to roll up your sleeves and get your hands dirty. And you make sure, as much as possible, that everything you do counts.

You're always watching for your moment, always preparing, putting in your 10,000 hours of practice[10] so you can take advantage of the moment that your hard work presents.

If you're a leader – and everyone who influences other people is a leader, title or no – you have to be willing to be out front, to be above the fray. But you also have to be willing to get in and help do the heavy lifting, because the work is urgent, because you're trying to send a signal to your followers, or because you're stopping to teach them a lesson.

If you're managing this paradox, you should be on *and* behind the stage. You're just as passionate about your work whether everyone sees it – or only you do.

TAKE FRESH ACTIONS TO LIVE THIS PARADOX

Describe a "movie star" you know. What do you like about his or her "celebrity"?

_____
_____
_____

Describe a "stagehand" you know. What do you like about his or her attitude and effort?

_____
_____
_____

Think of a "star" time in your life, even all the way back to your school years. What could you have done "behind the scenes" to make even more of that time, to get even more out of it?

_____

_____

_____

Remember a time when you were doing the hard work and others were getting all of the credit. What could you have done to put yourself in a position to "shine," to take advantage of time or circumstances and make a difference as a leader?

_____

_____

_____

A few will spend most of their lives in the spotlight, and many will spend most of their lives behind the spotlight.

Now you know the place to be – all around the spotlight. You want to be running it, or you want to be glowing in it. But you never, ever, want to be just standing there, lurking in the darkness or blocking the light.

A Long Line of Advisors

Michael Kairis was raised in a construction family and grew up visiting job sites with his father, Raymond, a strong, reserved man. The love of construction was something they shared. That passion ran so deep that Kairis says God must have breathed it into him when he was born.

When Kairis was little, his father would take him along on dump truck rides. His family indulged the boy with Tonka trucks, and friends gave him opportunities to do small projects for them.

As a junior in high school, Kairis enrolled in a program that allowed him to take classes in the morning and work in the afternoons two days a week. At his mother's urging, he decided to pursue veterinary medicine. A month passed, and the teacher told Kairis that she had called a parent/teacher conference. It was there that she informed his parents that while

Kairis was doing well in his class work, he had yet to visit the veterinarian's office. Following some discussion, the teacher suggested to his parents that they let him work at a small civil engineering company where he could assist engineers in testing steel, concrete, and masonry samples for a major bridge project being built in town.

"Not only did I work the required 2 afternoons a week, but I ultimately worked myself into a part-time position!" he recalls.

Kairis graduated and left for college with $7 to his name and everything he owned stuffed into a 1974 Oldsmobile. Four years later, he finished a degree in construction management, going on to pursue his dream in the industry.

Once he started a project, Kairis would focus with such intensity that he didn't eat or rest until he completed it. His passion for the work allowed him to "burn past the pain of hunger and fatigue." He worked all day as a field engineer on civil projects and then came home and worked into the night on an old house he and his wife purchased as a newly married couple.

"As I advanced in my career," he remembers, "I moved into the office, but I never lost my passion for the dirt, diesel, and steel of the field. I relished the salty, leathery old superintendents who took pride in their work and knew construction through decades of projects and untold pairs of steel-toed boots. I challenged myself to push past their 'no college boy is going to tell me what to do' attitude to earn their regard, breathing in any amount of wisdom and experience they had to offer me."

Over time, Kairis's combination of hard work and humility won him the right to lead.

"Once I understood that the ability to love, mentor, and win the trust of others was the secret to success in all vocations," he says, "I was able to thrive in my passion for building."

The results this approach has produced are obvious. Since working as a construction executive with some of the country's leading contractors and developers, including the Turner Construction Company, the Opus Group, and most recently as Vice President of Real Estate & Development with J.P. Morgan, Kairis, now President & CEO of Legacy Portion, LLC, still seeks to draw on the best of both executive and on-the-ground perspectives, and to learn from both older and younger workers even as he leads them. Managing these paradoxes, he believes, is the key to his success.

"Even as I've grown older, I value the input from the younger people," he says. "I think it comes across in my attitude of wanting to participate and still learn the business, even from the ground level. I also share my experiences down from the boardroom and become *unguarded, so they can manage up. It benefits both; it comes across as a shared mentorship. To take it one step farther, I seek out people who are older than me because it's important to be mentored as you continue your journey."*

Ultimately, the paradox of leading with humility means remembering your roots, Kairis argues. "When I don't hear the sounds of the backup alarms or the smell of fresh concrete, it's almost like a withdrawal," he says. "I want to have that be a part of my future life in leadership at the executive level because it reminds me of where I come from. Some people, when they get to a certain level, they want to be removed. I never viewed it that way. I felt like the people were important. Your understanding of new techniques, understanding day-to-day struggles—it helps you be a better leader, both professionally and spiritually."

PARADOX 3: LEARN FROM HISTORY AND LIVE IN THE MOMENT

FIVE PARADOXES FOR LIVING YOUR LIFE
  Be an Optimist and a Realist
  Be a Movie Star and a Stage Hand
> **LEARN FROM HISTORY AND LIVE IN THE MOMENT**
  Be a Leonardo and a Washington
  Be a Carnegie and a Scrooge

Learn from History

One of the hardest things to do in life is to accurately remember history, and it doesn't matter whether it's our personal history, the narrative of a relationship, or a project or decision-making review. There's often a lot of misery and pain back there, and it's easy to dismiss it as "old news."

But not learning from real history leads to enrollment in what we call the "School of Hard Knocks." Life keeps enrolling us in different courses, like "learning whom to trust," "using a blend of intuition and analysis," and "sharing power intelligently." If we don't pass, we get re-enrolled, and we have to keep taking the class until we either pass it or die.

> **"THOSE THAT FAIL TO LEARN FROM HISTORY ARE DOOMED TO REPEAT IT."**
> **WINSTON CHURCHILL, BRITISH PRIME MINISTER** [11]

Think about a big mistake made by your organization (no gloating here if you didn't contribute to it). What were the key things the organization should have learned from it? Put a percentage next to each one, highlighting how much of that lesson you think was actually learned.

Mistake:_____

Key Learning:

____% 1._____

____% 2._____

____% 3._____

Now do the same for yourself. This mistake can be personal or work-related (you'll learn lessons from either one that will improve the other category). If your percentages are low, note what you'll do to improve them.

Mistake:_____

Key Learning:

____% 1._____

____% 2._____

____% 3._____

There's treasure back there, riches that will buy you better thinking, actions, decisions, relationships, and success in your life to come.

"INSTILLING PASSION IS NOT SOMETHING THAT JUST OCCURS AT THE SPUR OF THE MOMENT. IT'S SORT OF A WAY OF LIFE."

FRED KOCHER, PRESIDENT & GENERAL MANAGER (RETIRED),

AAR CORPORATION

Live in the Moment

Some people spend their whole lives reliving the past. Who needs that?

The past can't really be relived, just regurgitated. The future is unknown and mostly outside of our control. But right now? That's gold.

"The earth belongs to the living," noted U.S. President Thomas Jefferson.[12] There is no moment to live in except the one you have right now. Successful, fulfilled people recognize this important little truth, and they work hard to extract everything they can out of what's in front of them.

> **"FOR PRESENT JOYS ARE MORE TO FLESH AND BLOOD THAN A DULL PROSPECT OF A DISTANT GOOD."**
>
> **JOHN DRYDEN, ENGLISH POET**

There are some ways to "live in the moment" badly. We can drink too much and ruin tomorrow (and maybe our livers). We can eat too much, forget how much the scales have depressed us, and spoil ten thousand future moments. What else are you doing in your life right now that is living *badly* in the moment?

1. _____
2. _____
3. _____

Now let's look at it from the other side. There are many ways to fill "now" to the full. You can send short emails or text messages of encouragement to one or more friends or coworkers every day. What else could you add into "now" that would make it come alive?

1. _____
2. _____
3. _____

There's living in the moment, and then there's robbing the moment. Passionate people learn the difference – and live it.

Live in the Past and the Present

Managing this paradox leads us to become *mindful forgetters*.

We don't ignore the past and its lessons. We make sure we go into the present fully armed. We refuse to let any useful lessons get away from us. We're careful to learn the *right* lessons. Otherwise, we'll cripple ourselves in the right now.

And then we let the specifics go. We remember the lessons, but not the "stuff" that taught them to us. We recall the lessons of history, but not the history.

It's said about American football great Joe Montana that he was able to make a bad play and then completely forget it before the next play. But this evaluation does him a disservice. Fans could tell from listening to him that he somehow remembered *everything that had been done wrong* – so he wouldn't let it happen again. He just didn't let the past cripple him emotionally in the *now*.

Passionate people, like Montana, work hard to forget the emotional downers from the past – *but never its lessons*.

People have been told for centuries that "the unexamined life is not worth living."[13] They've also been told, "don't think about it so much" and "forget the past." So which is it?

You know.

TAKE FRESH ACTIONS TO LIVE THIS PARADOX

Pick an event or situation from your life about which you could be a "mindful forgetter," of something that's been hard to face head on. What are the key details of this tough past?

_____
_____
_____

Now try to draw out one or more good lessons from this situation:

_____
_____
_____

Now think about where and how these lessons could be applied to make now even better:

_____
_____
_____

Finally, jot down a "mindful forgetter" summary, such as "I'll remember not to jump too fast into relational commitment, but I won't dwell on the relationship that taught me to take things slowly"; or "I'll be more careful in taking on that kind of work, but I won't obsess over memories of the 3 assignments that taught me to be careful":

_____
_____
_____

Learn from the past – and forget it: it's the very best way to live in the moment.

PARADOX 4: BE A LEONARDO AND A WASHINGTON

FIVE PARADOXES FOR LIVING YOUR LIFE
Be an Optimist and a Realist
Be a Movie Star and a Stage Hand
Learn from History and Live in the Moment
> **BE A LEONARDO AND A WASHINGTON**
Be a Carnegie and a Scrooge

Be a Leonardo

The ultimate Renaissance man, the embodiment of creativity, was Leonardo da Vinci. He painted, sculpted, designed, invented. He was interested in *everything*. He also saw the connections between everything. A sketch of a human being was at once both art and science. As Paul Johnson writes, "No one can say for sure whether he regarded painting an easel portrait like the *Mona Lisa* or the *Last Supper* wall painting in Milan, or designing an impregnable fortress as the thing he most wanted to do, or felt was most worth doing."[14]

You can be a Leonardo. It starts with being interested in everything. You read or watch programs outside of what "naturally" grabs you. You ask questions. You ponder how apparently unlike things are actually alike. There's so much out there that is captivating. When I (Jim) speak on leadership, I draw lessons and examples from history, biography, architecture, life sciences, social sciences, sports – the pieces of life make music when they're pulled together in creative ways.

Think about your personal interests. Jot down 3 that come to mind but are currently getting little or none of your time. Note one creative thing you could do to get each one moving.

1. _____
2. _____
3. _____

Now move onto your work and career. What could you learn, get cross-trained in, or simply start doing right where you are? How could you bring a breath of fresh air into these?

1. _____
2. _____
3. _____

Some people say, "I'm just not creative." But that's nonsense. We were all born "creative." It's just a matter of having the desire and will to go find that part of you again.

> **"YOU CAN'T DEPEND ON YOUR JUDGMENT WHEN YOUR IMAGINATION IS OUT OF FOCUS."**
> **MARK TWAIN, AUTHOR**[15]

Be a Washington

George Washington was there at the creation of the United States of America. But astoundingly creative he was not. He was instead the steady force, the disciplined core, the "plodder" who brought order out of revolution.

Being disciplined is, for most of us, a *huge* challenge. We may not even want it. We want freedom, not control! But the discipline we're talking about here is *self-discipline*. No one made Washington a person always under control; he did that for himself. And his discipline allowed him to achieve great things – far more than most of the highly creative people who have ever lived.

Today, this self-discipline might include only checking your email once or twice a day, and not before you've done some creative thinking that "emailitis" might destroy. What else could you reduce or eliminate, starting right now, to bring some needed self-discipline into your life and work?

1. _____
2. _____
3. _____

There may be some new actions you could take to enhance this area of your life. For instance, at Luman International, we don't schedule meetings with clients (or ourselves) before 10:00 a.m., so everyone has a chance to think about things before they start doing them. Where else could you or your team be proactive in self-discipline?

> "CONCENTRATE ALL YOUR THOUGHTS UPON THE WORK AT HAND. THE SUN'S RAYS DO NOT BURN UNTIL BROUGHT TO A FOCUS."
>
> ALEXANDER GRAHAM BELL, TELEPHONE INVENTOR[16]

1. _____
2. _____
3. _____

At the end of your life, you can look at a pile of creative "shouldas." *Or not.*

Be a Focused Instigator

If we're going to make anything around us even a little bit better, we'll need to be *disciplined creators*.

Creativity without discipline means that much of it will be wasted. Many creative projects will never get off the ground, and those that do will mostly not get finished. Leonardo, with all of his mighty creative genius, failed to capitalize on it. Johnson notes that "with such a range of interests, he lacked the ferocious concentration on any particular one, at any time, that his younger contemporary Michelangelo could bring to bear… Leonardo was a much more extreme case of the distracted and ill-disciplined polymath…. No one who saw anything done by him, even a mere drawing, failed to admire him…. But his final public output was meager."[17]

Discipline without creativity means that we continue to hone – and ultimately bore ourselves with – the narrow band of thinking and activity that we already own. We may do this or that well, but never even touch the rich collection of ideas and potential locked away in the attic of our minds.

How many creative types have failed because they lacked discipline? And how many people are so disciplined that they can't access their imaginations (and end up doing the wrong thing really well?[18])

We need to be creative *and* disciplined, and we need to marry the two in an intimate relationship if we want to get the most out of them both. We need to be creative polymaths like Leonardo, and we need to connect that creativity to a simple, focused plan for execution and follow through like Washington.

> **"'MUSIC DEPENDS ON DISCIPLINE,' JANIS SAYS. 'BUT IT ALSO DEPENDS ON FREEDOM.'"**
> **JEFFREY KLUGER, AUTHOR[19]**

The American Revolution needed the creative force of a Thomas Jefferson and a Thomas Paine *and* the steady hand of a George Washington.

When the concept of "octaves" was introduced centuries ago, many people thought this framework would be too restrictive. They pictured the death of musical creativity. What happened instead was an explosion of fresh work, as octaves provided enough structure – enough discipline – to make creativity safe. But discipline can't be taken too far. Music needs both math and soul.

TAKE FRESH ACTIONS TO LIVE THIS PARADOX

External control is stifling. Internal control is, ironically, the path to freedom – and genuine creativity. What external control do you need to shed so you can feel a release of freedom?

_____

_____

_____

What internal control could you start exercising right now that would directly open up some creative space for you?

_____

_____

_____

To be a disciplined creator, you first have to find an area of great interest to you:

_____

_____

_____

Now, what would you have to change, stop doing, or start doing, in both self-discipline and creativity, to give you a chance to make something of this important area?

_____

_____

_____

Think of what Leonardo could have done with a Washington to drive him to finish his work. Think of how weaknesses in the original U.S. Constitution could have been removed with a Leonardo to push George Washington, the convention chair. Controlled explosions might have occurred in both cases.

The Process of Paradox

For Rich Kucharski, leadership is an exercise in managing paradoxes. Now serving as a managing director of a business unit at a large tech company, Kucharski previously started his own company and worked in other firms, a range of experiences that give him insight into the strengths of both large and small organizations.

"The benefit of a large organization is that they have a lot of relationships with other companies on the technology side to get products qualified," he points out. "But one of the challenges that they face is that they have a very detailed process for doing it: 'We don't do things that way. This is how we do things.' And they may not announce a product until all areas are qualified – whereas a customer might be requesting just a small portion of the product."

Small firms often have strengths in product development and customer service, Kucharski observes.

At this tech company, Kucharski strives to embrace the best of both—the capacity and process strengths of a large organization and the agility of a small firm. "We're trying to be responsive to the customer's requirements. We're pushing to say, 'You know what,? We don't need this whole thing qualified. We just need this sliver. Let's support it.'"

Kucharski has done stints in organizations that are now customers of his present employer, a history that gives him perspective on their needs now that he's inside the storied organization. "The thing I always think about is, what's the right thing to do for the customer?" he says.

When internal processes might otherwise stand in the way of adapting quickly to a customer's needs, Kucharski tries to focus people on the value of small-firm flexibility. "I paint the picture for them: 'Here's what the customer's looking to do. Here's why this is important. Here's the commitment that we can make. Here's the value that we can get out of it.' People in this company see that, so that helps us push through the process."

It's an approach that Kucharksi recommends to leaders in organizations of all sizes. "You need to say, 'I understand the process. I'm not trying to break the process.' But just say, 'Here's what the customer's looking to do. Here's how we can help develop that. Here's how we can grow our revenue.'" Kucharski doesn't expect everyone to get it the first time, so he advises a bit of "thickheaded persistence": "When they say 'no,' call back and say, 'Hey, did I tell you about this customer?' And by the third, fourth, sixth time, I'm sure they'll say, 'This guy's a mental patient.' But you're able to get things moving in a different direction."

Kucharski has discovered another paradox he has to manage: communicating more often so he can save time. "Right now, I have about 50 to 60 people on my team globally," he explains. "So the challenge I have is talking to everybody, spending time with the leaders frequently. With constant communication, the person feels like I'm going to call them back the next day or the following day, so he's not trying to dump everything at once." This counterintuitive approach helps Kucharski move through a discussion of the day's project without getting slowed down by distractions or caught up in the details of another project.

Kucharski traces this lesson about the need for clarity to an unlikely source: a dive instructor he met when he went scuba diving several years ago. "When diving at night, you jump into water, you have your flashlight, and you just see millions of lights out in the water," he explains. "'If you try to look at all of them, you see millions of dots,'" he recalls the instructor saying, "'but if you focus in on one piece, you really start to see what's happening under the ocean.'" Kucharski applies the lesson to leadership: "As you try to understand the larger picture, don't attempt to focus on the whole picture. Focus on one thing, and the rest will come into focus. As you're looking at challenges that you're faced with in life, don't try to take on all of them at once. Focus on one area, get good at that, and move into the next area."

Paradoxically, Kucharski has found a way to focus on the short term and the long term at the same time. "We're quarterly focused. That's always in the backdrop. Depending on where you are in the quarter, you only have 90 days or less to get going," he says. "So I try to split my week with some amount of tactical ('we have to fix a problem today'), some amount of building to the quarter, but really focusing more on questions like, 'What are we doing next quarter? Who are we hiring for next quarter? How are we building the team? What training are we doing for next quarter?' I need to make sure I'm looking at next quarter because that will be here before we know it."

> **"THERE'S A UNIFIED PRESENTATION OF A VISION THAT AN ARTIST IS CAPABLE OF. GOOD ARTISTS DON'T 'THINK UP THINGS.' IF ONE HAS THE GIFT, YOU MUST ALLOW THE UNFETTERED FLOW OF INSPIRATION TO COME THROUGH YOU, AND CAPTURE IT AND EDIT IT INTO A FORM THAT'S PRESENTABLE. HOLLYWOOD IS THE EXACT OPPOSITE. IT'S ALL ABOUT PLOTS, OUTLINES, MEETINGS, AND JUSTIFICATIONS."**
>
> RODERICK TAYLOR, POET, SCREENWRITER, SONGWRITER

PARADOX 5: BE A CARNEGIE AND A SCROOGE

FIVE PARADOXES FOR LIVING YOUR LIFE
Be an Optimist and a Realist
Be a Movie Star and a Stage Hand
Learn from History and Live in the Moment
Be a Leonardo and a Washington
> **BE A CARNEGIE AND A SCROOGE**

Be a Carnegie

It's easy today for young people to sit in Carnegie Hall and have no idea of how it got its name.

Andrew Carnegie was one of the few giants of the industrial revolution. He built what became U.S. Steel and amassed an unimaginable amount of money. And then he gave it away. In his book *The Gospel of Wealth*, he encouraged everyone to follow his lead. Hundreds of libraries – and Carnegie Hall – exist because Andrew Carnegie gave away his money. He made a mockery of the old prejudice that Scots weren't generous.

> **"SURPLUS WEALTH IS A SACRED TRUST WHICH ITS POSSESSOR IS BOUND TO ADMINISTER IN HIS LIFETIME FOR THE GOOD OF THE COMMUNITY."**
> ANDREW CARNEGIE, PHILANTHROPIST[20]

Generosity is good for the soul. "It's more blessed to give than to receive," the proverb reminds us. And giving more is better than giving less. Magnanimous people – the word means "great heart" – don't give until it hurts. They give until it feels good.

There are a lot of things we can give to others, lots more than just money. You can let people pull ahead of you in traffic. You can let someone else present that point in a meeting. What could you start giving away – small things – today?

How would you describe a generous person? Write a short, focused description of a generous person you know, considering both character and actions:

_____

_____

_____

There's no way to make a difference, no way to really count, unless you affect other human beings. And the only way to do that is to give something of yourself away.

Be a Scrooge

Be a Scrooge? Are you kidding? Wasn't he the bad guy in Charles Dickens' famous novel *A Christmas Carol*?

Well, yes and no. Before his "conversion" on Christmas Eve, Scrooge was a very bad guy indeed. Cheap. Stingy. Worse, miserly. Clutching. Hoarding.

But Carnegie also didn't give away most of his wealth until late in life. Bill Gates didn't start his foundation as a young man, and Warren Buffet didn't contribute to it until he was elderly. Scrooge turned into a very, very good guy. He was extremely effective in helping others – *but only because he had so much to share*.

You can't give away what you don't have. Today, many of us are good accumulators like Scrooge, only we accumulate *debt* rather than *wealth*. We might have a lot of things, and not really own any of them. We want to be in a position to provide for ourselves, and not depend on our children and churches and governments. We want to purchase our own freedom, to do what we want when we want. And unless we have hearts of stone, we want enough that we can use some of it to give a boost to others along the way.

So is there anything that could be cut back – or out – in your personal life? Eating out, clothes, extra cable services? Could you let your children earn part or all of their own college expenses (also good for their character)? Pick 3, but only write them down if you intend to take action on them *now*.

1. _____

2. _____

3. _____

Think about your work or business. Is any of it asking for a little "Scrooge-like" accumulation?

1. _____
2. _____
3. _____

It's too easy to waste both a little and a lot along the way, and end up with nothing for yourself or others later. Fill up the tank with money and time so you can drive with true class and generosity to your very last day.

Be a Miserly Philanthropist

A lot of influence – and friends – await us, if we generally act like *tight-fisted givers*.

You can give so much away along the way that you have nothing to give away at all, or nothing big enough to really count.

> **"TIME IS THE SCARCEST RESOURCE, AND UNLESS IT IS MANAGED, NOTHING ELSE CAN BE MANAGED."**
> **PETER F. DRUCKER, MANAGEMENT EXPERT**[21]

The president of a large philanthropic foundation told me that most not-for-profit organizations had no sense of this truth: if they got a donation or support, they immediately spent it all. No saving, no investing, no building – no giving themselves an opportunity to make the really big difference.

But you can also hold on to things too long. That vacation you don't take with your family because it's too expensive, and then the kids are grown and gone. The years you could have enjoyed that family room with just a little remodeling. That "just thinking of you" present you decided not to give because there was no occasion that demanded it. Holding on to money too long can stain your fingers.

To manage this paradox, we have to know when to be generous (with money, time, commitment) and when to tighten up and give nothing. We have to distinguish the merely "okay" causes that can drain us from the truly great ones that can be game-changers. We learn to give nothing here so we can give more over there. We learn to save and invest now to multiply our impact later – whether that's a personal gift or a business investment in the future.[22]

TAKE FRESH ACTIONS TO LIVE THIS PARADOX

Describe a giver you know. What do you like about him or her that you could adopt?

_____
_____
_____
_____
_____

Describe a tight-fisted person you know. What does he or she do right that you could adopt?

_____
_____
_____
_____
_____

In your personal life, where could you reduce spending or time in one area to directly enhance another?

_____
_____
_____
_____
_____

And how about the same question in your work life? Where could you free up some funds or hours to power another idea or reward one of your "winners and believers?"

_____

_____

_____

The key lesson to learn from Scrooge is to spend little so you can give away a lot. The key lesson to learn from Carnegie is to do it.

"BY IMPROVING YOUR QUALITY, YOU REDUCE COSTS, AND BY REDUCING CYCLE TIME, YOU REDUCE COSTS. THE REAL FOCUS IS REDUCING COSTS, BUT THE WAY TO DO THAT IS TO IMPROVE QUALITY AND REDUCE CYCLE TIME."

JOHN BADE, PH.D., DIRECTOR, STRATEGIC DEVELOPMENT,
THE BOEING COMPANY

RELATING TO OTHERS – 5 PARODOXES

Now that you've spent some time considering the personal paradoxes that present themselves as you live your life—your life as a leader, as a family member, as a person—we'd like to invite you to consider 5 more. These 5 paradoxes lie at the center of how we relate to others.

PARADOX 1: MOVE FORWARD BOLDLY AND STOP FOR CORRECTION

FIVE PARADOXES FOR RELATING TO OTHERS
> MOVE FORWARD BOLDLY AND STOP FOR CORRECTION
  Get All Wrapped Up and Disentangle
  Expect Perfection and Expect Mistakes
  Give People the Maximum and Commute Their Sentences
  Be an Iron Fist and a Velvet Glove

Move Forward Boldly

"You miss 100 percent of the shots you don't take," said hockey great Wayne Gretzky.[23] Basketball star Charles Barkley noted that the only bad shots were the ones you missed. In other words, it doesn't matter if it looks good as long as the ball goes into the basket.

We've all heard about "analysis paralysis," but what about plain old *paralysis*? So many of the decisions that get mulled over and procrastinated on aren't being analyzed; they're being *anesthetized*. Many things can be decided with a 50 percent analysis, and some can be resolved with *no* analysis.

There is probably at least one thing in your personal life that's crying out for action. Start this relationship, end that one, try that church, join that group, dabble in that hobby. Describe your 'call for action' here:

_____

_____

_____

And at work, something has been clouding your mind or desk for a long time, or slowing your agenda, or stymieing your team. What will you do?

_____

_____

_____

Action isn't a substitute for thought, but thought isn't a substitute for action, either.

Stop for Correction

"I like to get input before I make a decision," a senior manager told me, "but after I make it, I want no more dialogue. I want everyone to get behind it without hesitation."

"But what if the decision is wrong?" I asked.

There are no perfect decisions. Leaders who think they've made them have bigger problems than the decisions they've made, no matter how bad those are. We have to make all of our decisions with less than perfect data and analysis. So why not face that reality, and make stopping for correction a way of life? Why not build it into the decision-making process?

Think about your personal life, and note a few things that could use a little search for imperfection:

> **"IN ORDER TO ATTAIN THE IMPOSSIBLE, ONE MUST ATTEMPT THE ABSURD."**
> **MIGUEL DE CERVANTES, AUTHOR**[24]

1. _____
2. _____
3. _____

And in your career or education, what has gone on for a long time that begs the powerful question, "Why on earth am I doing this?"

1. _____
2. _____
3. _____

Running a life or a career or a business is a lot like taking a vacation. It helps to know when and where to stop.

Be Determined to Stop and Go Fast

The way to a passionate, fulfilled life is to *drive fast and make the pit stops count*.

We make much better decisions and get much better overall results when we run as fast as we can – until we stop cold. A racing team optimizes its car to run as fast as it can, right up to the moment when it's in the pit and *not moving at all*.

Our "most-of-the-time" mode needs to be action. Keep things moving. Don't get stale. Learn what you absolutely need to know and then *act*.

But right from the start, build in personal and team *PitStops*™[26]: times planned in advance, so you don't let the wheels come off of yourself or your team.

Building in a stop could be as simple as setting a date when some things (or all things) are back on the table. Or it could include a series of pre-set meetings where you can make changes or improvements – or cancellations.

We have to be zealous about our mission – *and* we have to be open to correcting it.

> "IF YOU HAVE MADE MISTAKES, EVEN SERIOUS ONES, THERE IS ALWAYS ANOTHER CHANCE FOR YOU. WHAT WE CALL FAILURE IS NOT THE FALLING DOWN BUT THE STAYING DOWN."
>
> **MARY PICKFORD, ACTRESS**[25]

TAKE FRESH ACTIONS TO LIVE THIS PARADOX

Describe a hard-charger you know. What do you like about his or her bias towards action that you could adopt?

_____
_____
_____

Describe a cautious person you know. What do you like about his or her thoughtfulness that you could adopt?

_____
_____
_____

To win, you have to push forward into the unknown, and you have to try to see into the unknown as far and as deep as possible. Pick a situation in your life. What would you have to change in order to address it both more boldly and thoughtfully at the same time?

_____
_____
_____

A racecar that spends the race in the pit is guaranteed to finish out of the money. One that tries to race without stopping in the pit has the same guarantee – and might have the engine blow up to boot.

There are only two speeds in a passionate life – really fast, and standing still.

PARADOX 2: GET ALL WRAPPED UP AND DISENTANGLE

FIVE PARADOXES FOR RELATING TO OTHERS
Move Forward Boldly and Stop for Correction
> **GET ALL WRAPPED UP AND DISENTANGLE**
Expect Perfection and Expect Mistakes
Give People the Maximum and Commute Their Sentences
Be an Iron Fist and a Velvet Glove

Get All Wrapped Up

You just have to be involved.

Introvert, extrovert, shy, outgoing – it doesn't matter. If you want to make a difference, if you want to count, you have to be involved in the lives and work of other people.

If you're going to get all wrapped up with other people, there are some things you're going to have to avoid. You can't pry into personal matters over which you can have no influence. What are some other things you should avoid in your personal quest for involvement?

1. _____
2. _____
3. _____

> **"THERE'S A PASSION IN THE ENTERTAINMENT INDUSTRY. THERE'S AN ACCEPTANCE OF PEOPLE'S DIFFERENCES. IN THE INDUSTRY, YOU CAN DIG DEEP AND GET THE REAL TRUTH. PEOPLE ARE SO SCARED AND INTIMIDATED WHEN THEY AUDITION, AND I HAVE SUCH A PASSION FOR PEOPLE; I CAN BE MOTHERLY. THERE ISN'T ONE PERSON ON EARTH WHOM I DON'T FIND FASCINATING. I LIKE TO HELP THEM GET CLOSER TO FINDING HOPE AND TRUTH."**
> **HEIDI TUTTLE, CASTING AGENT**

But there are things you can do more to increase your involvement. You can keep a small notebook of personal information about your team members – their hobbies, kids' names and interests, favorite dessert – and bring those up in conversation. What else could you do?

1. _____
2. _____
3. _____

No one will really trust you unless they know you're somehow in the battle with them. They have to know you genuinely care. And then they'll fight for you.

"ALL PEOPLE LIVE, NOT BY REASON OF ANY CARE THEY HAVE FOR THEMSELVES, BUT BY THE LOVE FOR THEM THAT IS IN OTHER PEOPLE."

LEO TOLSTOY, AUTHOR[27]

Disentangle

What will you do to eliminate the influence of people who disturb your work, your effectiveness, your thoughts and feelings?

You can look up and be surprised at how involved you are in other peoples' problems. Why am I involved in their marital issues? What do I know that can really help them with their seriously messed-up child? When did I start listening to the everyday litany of complaints about their boss or work situation? Why do I find myself fixing and deciding things that I fully delegated to others?

When you're in the middle of a relationship that's draining the life out of you, or an ugly situation that you didn't create and don't own, it's time to disentangle. You're doing more harm than good, probably mostly to yourself. What do you need to drop like a bad habit?

1. _____
2. _____
3. _____

Most of us need to set up boundaries to prevent us from getting entangled in the first place. When someone asks for advice, we can give them one small thing to do, and have them get back to us for more when they've done it. This will eliminate the many who want to whine rather than win. What are other boundaries for you?

1. _____
2. _____
3. _____

Disentangling can be difficult, even traumatic. But that's a holiday compared with going down with someone else's ship.

> **"I BELIEVE MANAGING IS LIKE HOLDING A DOVE IN YOUR HAND. IF YOU HOLD IT TOO TIGHTLY, YOU KILL IT, BUT IF YOU HOLD IT TOO LOOSELY, YOU LOSE IT."**
> **TOMMY LASORDA, BASEBALL MANAGER**[28]

Sit Close, but Pull Down the Armrest

Your passion for people has a better chance of surviving if you become a *self-possessed bleeding heart*.

You have to start with the boundaries. It's a lot more difficult to establish limits when you're already entangled.

And then, with your boundaries in mind, throw yourself in. Get deeply involved. Let people know you really care and that you're in it for the long haul. If they press up against a boundary – like "I'll never give a second piece of advice to someone who has ignored the first one" – you back off. If they want to know what's wrong, you tell them. At some point – usually early – there's great value in making your boundaries known.

And if you slip up and find yourself fighting an octopus, you simply have to disentangle.

Leaders have to be involved with their troops but know when, how, and how much to stay aloof. They need to be involved from a distance. They don't want to compromise either their position *or* their relationships. They don't want to either care so much that they can't criticize, or criticize so much that others think they don't care.

There's nothing like closeness. Except space.

"PUSH UNTIL ALL IDEAS HAVE BEEN HEARD, RESPECTED, CONSIDERED, AND DECIDED."

CARY STOCKDELL, DIRECTOR, ORGANIZATIONAL DEVELOPMENT, SWIFT ENERGY

TAKE FRESH ACTIONS TO LIVE THIS PARADOX

Think about the person you know who is most involved with others, either at work or elsewhere. What is he or she doing that you would like to adopt?

_____
_____
_____

Now think about someone who is very good at keeping a healthy distance. What is he or she doing? Is there something there that you could do or mold a bit to fit your personality?

_____
_____
_____

Now pick one of your personal relationships that's weaker either on involvement or on boundaries than you'd like. What do you need to do to make this paradox come alive here?

_____
_____
_____

Now do the same with one of your work relationships – boss, colleague, subordinate. How can you get this paradox working for you?

_____
_____
_____

People who are fully passionate are passionate about people. But not all of them – and not all the time.

PARADOX 3: EXPECT PERFECTION AND EXPECT MISTAKES

FIVE PARADOXES FOR RELATING TO OTHERS
Move Forward Boldly and Stop for Correction
Get All Wrapped Up and Disentangle
> **EXPECT PERFECTION AND EXPECT MISTAKES**
Give People the Maximum and Commute Their Sentences
Be an Iron Fist and a Velvet Glove

Expect Perfection

We're "only human," as the saying goes. And if we aren't careful, this will be a perfectly agreeable reason to let mediocrity through the door for a very long visit.

If we're being honest, we have to admit that mediocrity is the norm in life: "It's good enough," "It's the best I can do," "Well, I tried" (as if trying counts for something if separated from results). Takeout orders with the wrong food, "customer service" people who don't care about customers *or* service, incomprehensible instruction manuals, surgical procedures that create more problems than they solve, shoddy construction and products, quality programs that stifle innovation which could actually improve quality - when you see something that's just above average, it can *seem* like perfection compared with the junk that surrounds it.

If you make room for something less than perfection, you will likely end up with something *far* less than perfection. Entropy takes over. Things deteriorate. The bar gets lowered. Pretty soon, you're just fighting for competence.

> **"CHASE PERFECTION. SETTLE FOR EXCELLENCE ALONG THE WAY."**
> **VINCE LOMBARDI, SPORTS LEGEND**[29]

So think about your work. Pick something that's right now on the "we're no worse than anyone else" scale. Then jot down a few thoughts about how you could start driving this toward passionate perfection.

Project, assignment, or task: _____

What I can do: _____

_____

Few people ever deliver a perfect report, or come up with a perfect strategy, or play a perfect game. But a few do. And if they can, so can you.

Expect Mistakes

There are so many ways to make mistakes – and sometimes people can find *all* of them.

We can blame a lot of these mistakes on things like poor strategies, overbearing policies and procedures, organizational hierarchy and politics, and a host of other "systemic" issues. But the problem is that *all of these mistake-ridden areas were created by people*. If you find a mistake of any kind and scratch below the surface, you'll find a human being.

So we might as well expect mistakes, because we're going to get them whether we expect them or not. But there's more. Mistakes can actually be a very valuable commodity. Whenever I (Jim) ask audiences, "How many of you have learned more from your failures than your successes?" almost every hand in the room goes up. Mistakes shouldn't have such a bad reputation. They're a key to learning and growth.

But to expect mistakes in a healthy way, there are certain things you have to eliminate. There are "good" mistakes, and there are "bad" mistakes (like sending a document out without proofreading or spellchecking it). What are some other "bad" mistakes?

1. _____
2. _____
3. _____

But you might as well take advantage of this whole mistake business. Where could you push your team to explore some new ways of doing things and make some *intelligent mistakes*™?

1. _____
2. _____
3. _____

It's hard to be passionate when every mistake brings the death penalty. Passionate leaders know the importance of building a risk-friendly, mistake-friendly culture.

> "I HAVE LEARNED THROUGHOUT MY LIFE AS A COMPOSER CHIEFLY THROUGH MY MISTAKES AND PURSUITS OF FALSE ASSUMPTIONS, NOT BY MY EXPOSURE TO FOUNTS OF WISDOM AND KNOWLEDGE."
>
> **IGOR STRAVINSKY**

Be Very Understanding and Very Demanding

Managing this paradox pushes us to become *tolerant perfectionists*.

You begin with the understanding that mistakes are going to happen, probably a lot. You give people a comfort zone where it's safe to try things, instead of giving them a reason to do as little as possible because more work means more mistakes and more punishment.

But you don't stop there. You want these mistakes to work for you. You want to mine every ounce of value out of them. You tell people to try. You say that you aren't tolerant of sloppiness, but you're *very* tolerant of intelligent efforts at improving… everything. You and your team begin to see every good mistake as *part of the process of moving toward perfection*.

It has become very commonplace for people to talk about "core competencies" – what do we do with some degree of skill? This is fine, but insufficient. We have to eliminate the activities at which we're really bad – at Luman International we call them *core incompetencies*™ – and spend more and more of our energy on activities at which we're really good – our *core excellencies*™.

Get rid of the stuff that is regularly producing mistakes (most of them bad) and embrace the trying (and sometimes failing) that gives you a shot at perfection.

> **"WE HAVE ENOUGH STRESS IN OUR OFFICE JUST BY THE NATURE OF THE BUSINESS, SO WE DON'T CREATE FALSE STRESS. WE ARE VERY TASK-ORIENTED, NOT 'LET'S JUST PUT IN AN HOUR TO IMPRESS SOMEBODY.'"**
>
> **GARY FROSSARD, PRESIDENT & CEO, KADEAN CONSTRUCTION**

TAKE FRESH ACTIONS TO LIVE THIS PARADOX

What could you do to create a safety zone for your team so they can fail their way to perfection?

_____

_____

_____

Describe a recent or current problematic, mistake-ridden situation. What could you learn from it to turn into future gold?

_____

_____

_____

Describe some of your organization's *core incompetencies*™ and how you could minimize them or their effects.

1. _____
2. _____
3. _____

Now describe some of your organization's *core excellencies*™ and how you could maximize their impact.

1. _____
2. _____
3. _____

PARADOX 4: GIVE PEOPLE THE MAXIMUM AND COMMUTE THEIR SENTENCES

FIVE PARADOXES FOR RELATING TO OTHERS
Move Forward Boldly and Stop for Correction
Get All Wrapped Up and Disentangle
Expect Perfection and Expect Mistakes
> GIVE PEOPLE THE MAXIMUM AND COMMUTE THEIR SENTENCES
Be an Iron Fist and a Velvet Glove

Give People the Maximum

Over a very long time in business, I (Jim) have cut a lot of people slack.

Sometimes they just seem to have so much *potential*. They have energy or talent or skills or experience or all of the above. But they just don't deliver the goods. The results aren't there. At first, you listen to excuses. Maybe you even *make* excuses for them – after all, you hired them so they must not be too bad, right? (You also don't want to admit you made yet another hiring or "management" mistake). But it always turns out badly.

Often, there's a character issue. Character is behind the scenes, but its effects always play out on stage. Maybe the person is lazy. Lacking self-discipline. Likes to party too much. Their personal life is in ruin. You will never fix them. As my friend Pete Luongo says, "You can help make them more than they are, but you can't make them different than they are."

Look around at your team, all the way down to the front lines. Where have you wasted a lot of good energy? Who needs to have their roles changed or reduced? Who needs to go?

1. _____

2. _____

3. _____

What are the warning signs that they could destroy your team or results? It might be showing up late, or turning in late reports, or making an inappropriate comment in a meeting. What might your "red alerts" look like going forward?

"CONFRONTATION SIMPLY MEANS MEETING THE TRUTH HEAD-ON."
MIKE KRZYZEWSKI, BASKETBALL COACH[30]

1. _____
2. _____
3. _____

Stop suffering fools gladly. Don't let them kill the passion of your team.

Commute Their Sentences

No question about it – you can have a "one and done," "win or go home," "sudden death" organizational culture.

There are a lot of problems with that culture, though. You'll lose a lot of good people who just missed it – maybe because of other people, bad information, poor delegation from above, a host of things outside their control. You'll create a "no mercy" environment that will encourage cutthroat competition even as it stifles fresh thinking, innovation, and teamwork. You, of course, will be feared – and probably hated as well.

In the right circumstances, commuting people's sentences – giving them better, even different than they deserve – can take them to a higher level of commitment. They'll have been given one of the best of all gifts, the second chance. Think of someone who could use a reprieve, and describe how you'd go about it:

_____
_____
_____

You'll need to set some boundaries around these commutations, however, or some people are going to take advantage of you. This might mean a "3-strike" rule – a big miss on the third time on a significant assignment and they're out. What might your commutation boundaries be?

1. _____
2. _____
3. _____

Mercy in work situations is often in short supply. If you offer it in appropriate situations, you've just given yourself one more competitive advantage in your quest for a passionate team.

"THE WEAK CAN NEVER FORGIVE. FORGIVENESS IS THE ATTRIBUTE OF THE STRONG."

MAHATMA GANDHI

Be a Take-No-Prisoners Liberator

Living a full, rich life is a lot more likely if we become *merciful stewards*.

Anyone in leadership has to start with being a steward – someone who is accountable for how the organization's resources are spent (or wasted). Some people are going to waste a lot (including our time) and possibly even harm the future of the organization. But the expectation has to be that everyone will contribute. If they don't, they're just taking up space, making others clean up their messes, and generally creating an unfair situation for all involved.

The problem is that early on, it's hard to tell the difference between one of these people and someone who is just having growing pains and making honest (if still unpleasant) mistakes. So this paradox moves us toward giving people considerable slack at the beginning, but then tightening it up very quickly.

Slack and mercy are invitations by a leader to learn and grow and do better. But we have to watch how people respond. Some people are dense, and take the absence of discipline or punishment as a lucky break rather than as an opportunity. The slack can end up enabling their bad behavior, and they might not even realize that they were actually chastised *before* they were reprieved. The lesson is to commute sentences *only as long as the behavior and results improve.*

But this approach would be appropriate only for technical, not ethical, errors. If there's a problem of skill or experience or communication, we can and should be quite merciful and hand out sentences slowly. But if there's a character issue, we should give the offender little or no slack: none if the failure is clear, a very small amount if it isn't. Even good results will turn south and eventually crash if they've arisen out of a character problem. Bad character keeps baseball players out of the Hall of Fame no matter how talented they were or what kind of results they delivered.

You should keep bad characters out of your building, too.

TAKE FRESH ACTIONS TO LIVE THIS PARADOX

Describe a tough disciplinarian you know. What do you like about his or her talk and actions that you could adopt?

_____

_____

_____

Describe a patient, forgiving person you know. What do you like about his or her talk and actions that you could adopt?

_____

_____

_____

How is managing this paradox different from the typical "discipline" approach?

_____

_____

_____

How would you apply this paradox with a new recruit?

_____

_____

_____

You can't put everyone in prison, and you can't let everyone out. Now you know how to make the call.

Leading with Inspiring Integrity

Bill Shumard is the President and CEO of Special Olympics Southern California (SOSC), an organization that serves more than 11,000 children and adults with disabilities.

A wealth of prior experience prepared Shumard to handle his position at SOSC. Prior to being named to his current position, he spent 10 years as Athletic Director at California State University, Long Beach (CSULB), where he was the second-longest tenured Athletic Director in the university's history, improving the university's NCAA graduation rate from 17 percent to 53 percent and raising over $7 million for capital improvements to athletic facilities.

Shumard remembers an early opportunity to practice integrity even at a cost.

"The men's volleyball coach — Alan Knipe, now the coach of the U.S. Men's Olympic Team — came to my office one day, saying, 'I'm going to have to suspend our star player for the game this Thursday. It has nothing to do with academics or breaking the law; it's more a moral or ethical issue. He did something his teammates thought was really, really wrong.'"

Shumard had emphasized his core value of integrity in earlier conversations with the coaches, but this was a chance to put it to the test. "I'm thinking, But we're playing UCLA Thursday night! Couldn't you do it against some second-tier team?" he says. "But even after pulling him out of the game, we ended up upsetting UCLA in the game. That was a great week."

The combination of performance-driven effort and unshakeable integrity inspired the people around Shumard.

"After making an unpopular decision to let someone go, I got killed in the press for it. This young guy on my staff came to me and said, 'I want you to know, I wouldn't give your job to a dog. I never wanted to be an athletic director. Until today. Watching how you stood tall and handled all this and still did the right thing—I want to be an athletic director now.' Someone from the inside seeing that you're right and saying, 'That was tough, but that was the right thing to do'—you're making a difference."

"It's always tough to make a controversial, confidential decision," Shumard admits. "But at the end of the day, the only thing you have left is your integrity and your reputation. Do people trust you or not? That's the bottom line."

PARADOX 5: BE AN IRON FIST AND A VELVET GLOVE

FIVE PARADOXES FOR RELATING TO OTHERS
Move Forward Boldly and Stop for Correction
Get All Wrapped Up and Disentangle
Expect Perfection and Expect Mistakes
Give People the Maximum and Commute Their Sentences
> **BE AN IRON FIST AND A VELVET GLOVE**

Be an Iron Fist

The longer you live and work with people, the more you see how easy it is for them to miss what you're saying. It can seem like no matter how hard you try, some just won't "get it."

President Harry Truman once said that if you wanted to get the attention of a Missouri mule, you had to hit it between the eyes with a board. On important points, you have to leave a mark. You can't gently "tap" the people who are having trouble listening; you have to communicate firmly and clearly. When they look in the mirror – *every* time they look in the mirror – they have to see that "mark" and remember what it means.

What person or team in your life is still not getting it, even after repeated attempts on your part? Write down what you would say if you were going to make it memorably (but not nastily) clear:

_____

_____

_____

There are specific things you can do to leave an impression, like having people repeat back to you in their own words what they think you just asked them to do. What else comes to mind? How could you consistently leave people with no room for misunderstanding?

1. _____
2. _____
3. _____

Communication that doesn't leave an impression is communication that can be deleted. Talk strongly – and you won't have to carry a big stick.

"PUT IT BEFORE THEM BRIEFLY SO THEY WILL READ IT, CLEARLY SO THEY WILL APPRECIATE IT, PICTURESQUELY SO THEY WILL REMEMBER IT, AND ABOVE ALL, ACCURATELY SO THEY WILL BE GUIDED BY ITS LIGHT."

JOSEPH PULITZER, JOURNALIST[31]

Be a Velvet Glove

Unless you say things in such a way that people want to hear them, there may be transmission of a message but there won't be much (if any) reception.

You can present your message with a velvet glove. Doing so tells the person on the receiving end, "I respect you. I know you're on the team and don't have to be bullied to understand what I'm saying." If you communicate with velvet, you'll get a level of attention and response that shouting and bullying can never command.

Who in your life has been pounded – by other people, by circumstances, by you? What could you say now that would be honest, but would still have the grace of velvet?

> "TREAT PEOPLE AS IF THEY WERE WHAT THEY OUGHT TO BE, AND YOU HELP THEM TO BECOME WHAT THEY ARE CAPABLE OF BEING."
>
> JOHANN WOLFGANG VON GOETHE, AUTHOR[32]

_____

_____

_____

Most people need a velvet glove, and they need it most of the time. It could be saying at the end of a delegation meeting, "What do you think?" or "Anything I've missed?" What could you build into your communication on a regular basis that would have a feel of velvet?

1. _____
2. _____
3. _____

Life and work have a lot of hard edges. You can be the velvet. If you are, you can watch the passionate commitment grow.

Be an Iron Fist in a Velvet Glove

Brutal leaders can get results, and kindhearted leaders can get commitment. If you want both results *and* commitment, though, you'll need to be a *hard-hitting ally*.

This paradox is different from the previous one, which concerned how to deal with things like mistakes, sloppiness, and unnecessary risk. This paradox addresses when and how to be a tough-minded leader and when to be benign – and as much as possible, to be tough-minded and benign at the same time.

You have to be clear, or you'll end up with a lot of people doing whatever they want to do, regardless of how it conflicts with what you said. It might be that they just didn't understand, but it could also be because they want to do something else and you're collaborating by being too unclear or too fast.

And you have to be kind, or people will do what you want – sort of – right up to the moment when they can escape. Fear works, but not forever. Fear works, but scared people won't. Harshness is perfectly designed to get a backlash, to have people slip across the border or stay on and sabotage the effort.

> "MY EXPERIENCE IS THAT PEOPLE GENERALLY WILL EXCEED YOUR EXPECTATIONS IF YOU GIVE THEM THE OPPORTUNITY TO SHOW YOU WHAT THEY CAN DO."
>
> **DON VARDEMAN, VP, WORLDWIDE FACILITIES, ANADARKO**

This is the way I (Jim) have said this to thousands of leaders: Be clear *and* be kind. The most powerful communication is blunt and subtle, unmistakable but palatable, startling but deeply resonating. Never communicate without the iron fist – but never forget to wear the velvet glove.

TAKE FRESH ACTIONS TO LIVE THIS PARADOX

Think about one of your own flaws. If someone were going to approach you with an iron fist in a velvet glove, what would this conversation sound like?

_____

_____

_____

Think about someone in your personal life with whom your communication has been lacking either the iron fist or the velvet glove (or both). Pick your most important message, and write it down here in your best "clear and kind" mode:

_____

_____

_____

Now try the same thing with someone at work — co-worker, subordinate, or even your boss:

_____

_____

_____

Joan of Arc and Mother Teresa. The Duke of Wellington and Mr. Rogers. Put them together, and you really have something.

"WE MUST COMBINE THE TOUGHNESS OF THE SERPENT WITH THE SOFTNESS OF THE DOVE, A TOUGH MIND AND A TENDER HEART."

DR. MARTIN LUTHER KING, JR.

PRODUCING BETTER PERFORMANCE – 5 PARADOXES

Living our lives and relating to others paradoxically opens the way to new heights of leadership. In this section, we'll explore 5 paradoxes for turning that leadership into results.

PARADOX 1: BE A ROCK AND A STREAM

FIVE PARADOXES FOR PRODUCING BETTER PERFORMANCE
> BE A ROCK AND A STREAM
Eliminate Distractions and Listen for Input
Throw the Dice and Use the Safe
Be a Racehorse and a Plow Horse
Push Hard and Cut Way Back

Be a Rock

Good leaders stand for something. Great leaders stand passionately for principle — like an unmovable rock, as Thomas Jefferson described it.[33]

If there isn't something at your core that you believe in, something that drives you in your work with other people, then whatever else you are, you aren't a leader. Leaders don't exist to give orders. What they do is give followers something to care about, something that lets them know that it isn't just "work" but rather is a *mission*.

Great, passionate leaders have a handful of non-negotiable, effective principles, like this core principle of integrity: "It's *never* the wrong time to do the right thing." What are your rock-solid principles – the things that can't be bought and that you won't ever sell?

1. _____
2. _____
3. _____
4. _____

This one may require a bit of soul-searching. Think back over your life, your education, your work. Think about the people of far-reaching influence. What were their non-negotiables? And how could you adopt these principles?

1. _____
2. _____
3. _____

Pragmatism can be a good thing, but nobody ever got called "passionate" or "great" because they were pragmatic alone. If you want those words attached to you, be a rock.

Be a Stream

Jefferson also reminded us, in matters of taste, to be like a stream.[35] As much as possible, go with the flow.

> "IF PRINCIPLE IS GOOD FOR ANYTHING, IT IS WORTH LIVING UP TO."
>
> BENJAMIN FRANKLIN, INVENTOR AND AMERICAN STATESMAN[34]

There really are things worth fighting for, but most of the fighting that human beings do isn't on the list. People fight about titles, sizes of offices, furniture, personal "slights" like not being copied on a memo or invited to a meeting. They fight about even bigger things – turf, information flow, approvals and sign-offs – that are also not worth fighting about. We can fight for all of this and more very passionately, but that behavior is an abuse of passion.

We have to give it up. We have to identify what isn't important, and let other people waste their energy on that. What low-value or worthless things do you see people fighting about in your organization – things that you want to avoid like a plague?

1. _____
2. _____
3. _____

Now let's take a deep breath and bring it closer to home. What are some of your pet projects or ideas that might not be worth your being a rock? Where or how could you go with the flow?

1. _____
2. _____
3. _____

Someone once said that we can spend our time trying either to move molehills a mile or mountains an inch. Give up the molehills. If you want to move mountains and you want others to join you willingly in the effort, you mostly have to be a stream.

"NOTHING IN THE WORLD IS MORE FLEXIBLE AND YIELDING THAN WATER. YET WHEN IT ATTACKS THE FIRM AND THE STRONG, NONE CAN WITHSTAND IT, BECAUSE THEY HAVE NO WAY TO CHANGE IT. SO THE FLEXIBLE OVERCOME THE ADAMANT, THE YIELDING OVERCOME THE FORCEFUL."

LAO-TZU, PHILOSOPHER[36]

Be a Moveable Monument

Our passion will really make a difference if we choose to be *occasional anchors*.

First, we have to decide what our anchors are. We don't want to be like the leader whose people would follow him anywhere – but only out of a sense of morbid curiosity. We have to know what makes a good and passionate leader.

But then we have to move that knowledge to the background. It's always there, guiding us, driving us, informing our thinking and decisions and actions. But we're not making it a battering ram, something so strong that we can't see any subtleties in its application or room for people to see things a bit differently. If one of our "rocks" is, "You always keep the boss informed about everything," we are in great danger unless we provide some nuance: if we're the boss, we'll drown in information, find ourselves majoring on the minor, end up with a lot of "reverse delegation," and have a lot of followers who spend a lot of time informing and not much time doing.

And beyond the non-negotiables, we have to let the fight go. We can't let ourselves spend time on these things, worry about them, fight about them. And we can't let our troops embroil us in their petty activities or warfare.

Let each person have his or her own "rocks" – areas that they care about deeply and passionately. If it's our rock, we stand firm as necessary and even make a big fuss about it. And (in general) if it's their rock, we let them have their way: we go with the flow and amaze them with our flexibility.

> "WE REALLY CONVINCED PEOPLE—STAFF, THEN CONSUMERS, THEN THE COMMUNITY—THAT WE WERE SERIOUS ABOUT THE MISSION AND THAT WE WERE SERIOUS ABOUT THE VALUES. IN OUR EVALUATIONS, IT WASN'T ONLY, 'HOW MANY PEOPLE DID YOU SERVE?' BUT IT WAS ALSO, 'DOES THIS PERSON ACTUALLY EXEMPLIFY THE VISION AND VALUES THAT WE HAVE ALL AGREED TO?'"
>
> **JAMES B. DESTEFANO,**
> **PRESIDENT & CEO,**
> **OCCUPATIONS, INC.**

TAKE FRESH ACTIONS TO LIVE THIS PARADOX

Describe a "rock" you know. What do you like about his or her unwillingness to yield that you could adopt?

_____
_____
_____

Describe a "stream" you know. What do you like about his or her flexibility that you could adopt?

_____
_____
_____

Where could you do a "stream for rock" trade?

_____
_____
_____

On the other side, you can stand firm on your "rocks" and force others to become "streams" in those areas. Where could a "show of strength" cause movement in one or more team members?

_____
_____
_____

If we know what should be immoveable – perhaps the vision, the values, the strategy – and what to flexify – possibly the tactics, the processes, the methods – we'll stir passion and performance all around.

PARADOX 2: ELIMINATE DISTRACTIONS AND LISTEN FOR INPUT

FIVE PARADOXES FOR PRODUCING BETTER PERFORMANCE
  Be a Rock and a Stream
> **ELIMINATE DISTRACTIONS AND LISTEN FOR INPUT**
  Throw the Dice and Use the Safe
  Be a Racehorse and a Plow Horse
  Push Hard and Cut Way Back

Eliminate Distractions

Distractions are like weeds that "ugly up" your yard or garden and eventually ruin it. And like weeds, they can't really be eliminated "once and for all"; you have to be diligent in weeding your yard again and again. Even better is preventing (as much as possible) the weeds from taking root in the first place.

The problem really isn't the easy-to-see distractions, like junk email and unannounced sales calls. We can put up barriers against those annoyances pretty easily. It's much more difficult to deal with the hard-to-discern distractions, like invitations to review low-impact reports, attendance at theoretically important regular meetings that never produce meaningful action, or requests to make decisions on things where we have competence but we *also* have someone two levels down who should be making the decision. We have to recognize these things as distractions and then eliminate them.

So let's start small. What are some easy-to-see distractions that you could take action on now? And what will you do to weed them out?

1. _____
2. _____
3. _____

And now for a harder question. What are you involved in or being asked to do that seems important on the surface but absolutely does not make a significant difference? And what will you do to kill these bigger weeds?

1. _____
2. _____
3. _____

Great leaders have been distracted all the way to incompetence. Great organizations have been distracted to death. Eliminate the distractions before they eliminate you.

Listen for Input

Sometimes – maybe a lot of the time – we can't hear the important stuff because we're being distracted.

And sometimes we're just not *listening*. Hearing is hard. Listening is harder.

But *really* listening is a cure for a lot of ills: half-baked decisions, strategies that look brilliant because we can't see the problems, hiring people who don't perform and then damage the team. In Luman's experience of uncovering issues with its clients, we find that almost every problem could have been eliminated or reduced in its impact, if only the listening had been broader and deeper.

But you can't listen to everyone on every topic. You have to have some listening "rules of the road," like "I will only listen to a complaint or problem if a person has at least two possible and legitimate solutions." Time to jot down your "rules":

1. _____
2. _____
3. _____
4. _____

You also have to think about possible new places to listen, like going along on some sales calls or taking the service department or production people to lunch. Leaders need listening strategies. What or where are yours?

1. _____
2. _____
3. _____
4. _____

It's easy to spend your life disillusioned and acting on bad information. If you want to make good decisions, be a passionate listener.

> **"TELL ME TO WHAT YOU PAY ATTENTION AND I WILL TELL YOU WHO YOU ARE."**
> **JOSÉ ORTEGA Y GASSET, AUTHOR**[37]

Be All Ears with Earplugs

We have to be careful how we listen. We need to be *focused wanderers*.

We have to start by deciding what's important to hear and absorb. What do we need to hear - what critical piece of information - from a team member, customer, non-customer, partner, instructor, consultant, contractor, or vendor? What value-creating gems of information or knowledge or wisdom are out there, waiting for us to dig them up?

> "REAL LISTENING IS A WILLINGNESS TO LET THE OTHER PERSON CHANGE YOU."
>
> ALAN ALDA, ACTOR AND AUTHOR[38]

And then we have to set up the means and mechanisms to hear those things often and well. Some things grow out of one-on-one conversations that would never be heard in a large meeting. Other things grow out of well-constructed team dialogue that an individual might feel too unprotected to share. The choice of forum often determines what we'll actually hear, so that choice is critical.

We have to wander outside the normal channels, which are usually too clogged up for anything useful to get through anyway.

And then we have to look at what's left. We listen for first things only, not just first, and then we reduce or eliminate all of the rest. We have our antennae out, but pointed in very specific directions. We filter out all of the white noise so we can really listen to what is truly meaningful.

TAKE FRESH ACTIONS TO LIVE THIS PARADOX

The worst distractions occur when we most need to focus. Think of a critical meeting or project. What kinds of things come up that are sort of related but really not important? How could those be weeded out?

_____

_____

_____

Sometimes we use distractions to keep us from having that difficult conversation or digging into an ugly problem. What are your "distraction escape hatches?" How can you avoid them?

_____

_____

_____

What are some forums you can set up to help you listen to what you need to hear?

1. _____
2. _____
3. _____

Stay focused? Keep our ears open? You can do both – but only with a passionate plan.

"I TELL FOLKS THAT WHEN WE ARE IN A ROOM OR ON A TEAM AND WE ALL HAVE THE SAME IDEAS, THEN WE ARE NOT MUCH OF A TEAM. SO THE REAL STRENGTH IS MAKING SPECIAL EFFORTS TO DRAW OUT NOVEL IDEAS THAT MAY NOT BE THE WAY I THINK AS THE LEADER."

DAN COLE, SENIOR VP, ADMINISTRATION,
AMAREN ENERGY, FUELS, & SERVICES

Anchoring the News and the Dinner Table

As a former radio show host and an award-winning TV news anchor and reporter, Julienne Smith-Chené was professionally trained as an effective communicator, yet she struggled to initiate substantial conversation at her own family table. Frustrated, Smith-Chené embarked on a quest to improve dinner conversation. Like the reporter she was, she kept a running notebook of deeper questions and meaningful talking points to stimulate discussions with her family.

"I started jotting down song lyrics and quotes from magazine articles, and I would use these as conversation starters at dinner that night," she says.

At first, the idea of re-engineering dinner proved a challenge.

"In the beginning, it was a little awkward because no one was really talking or sharing. I discovered that conversation is a learned art," Smith-Chené observes. "I have three children, and we were running in a million different directions. We made the decision to do family differently. We learned to slow down, and it has paid off in spades."

The enterprise grew out of Smith-Chené's childhood memories of spirited dinner conversation and often paradoxical pairings of guests.

"I grew up in a home where my father was a minister and an attorney," she recalls. "He had two doctorates. My parents made the decision that family meal time would be a priority. Those are some of my greatest family memories, even more than vacations. We had all sorts of interesting people around the dinner table with us: judges, homeless people—the conversations and connections were astounding."

Eventually, Smith-Chené collected the conversation starters she had accumulated into the best-selling, award-winning Food for Talk series. She remembers a vivid example of how using the materials opened a window into her children's thoughts.

"There's a question in the box that asks, 'What are some things that you dream? What is your most recent dream?' My son is rather quiet, and he shared his dreams about being able to fly without wings."

Smith-Chené has discovered some keys to sparking a good family conversation: "Give everyone at the table an opportunity to speak," she tells parents. "There are no right or wrong answers; this is just sharing your thoughts and ideas. Don't belittle anyone. Sometimes you need to give people a few seconds or minutes to collect their thoughts, even if there's silence. You have to be open to new ideas and opinions."

What started as a personal quest has become a cause for Smith-Chené.

"What I am really passionate about is encouraging moms and dads to bring back family dinner time into their homes," she explains. "Kids who eat a family meal four or more times a week are at half the risk of using drugs and alcohol, get better grades in school, are less at risk for suicide and depression, have fewer behavioral problems reported in school, and are at half the risk for obesity and weight problems."

For Smith-Chené, a lot of life boils down to doing the most effective thing at the most effective time and managing the paradox of immediate and long-term goals.

"Be very intentional with your life," she advises. "We must say 'no' to many things in order to be able to say 'yes' to the better things for our lives and families. It is possible to not live a harried life if you're willing to set clear goals. Someone told me, 'You only have your kids in your house for 18, 19, 20 years. That is only a short season in your life.' Realize that there will be seasons in the future when you can pursue those other things. You'll have plenty of time later."

PARADOX 3: THROW THE DICE AND USE THE SAFE

FIVE PARADOXES FOR PRODUCING BETTER PERFORMANCE
   Be a Rock and a Stream
   Eliminate Distractions and Listen for Input
> **THROW THE DICE AND USE THE SAFE**
   Be a Racehorse and a Plow Horse
   Push Hard and Cut Way Back

Throw the Dice

The biggest gamble of all is refusing to take *any* gambles. This seems safe, but what you're really doing is putting your plans and choices and future in the hands of others.

Throwing the dice doesn't mean just taking wild chances (although a few of those in a long life are probably a good thing). It means trying something *even if it seems like the odds are against you.* Maybe that client or customer won't take your call or call you back. Maybe no publisher will even look at your manuscript. Maybe your new idea will be shot down. But it doesn't matter. If you believe in it, you can try it. You *should* try it.

So let's start small. You could read a different genre of book, or take in a new television or radio program that you just *know* you're not going to like. Think about and jot down just a few small chances that you could take in the next few weeks:

1. _____
2. _____
3. _____

And now, let's try just a few bigger rolls of the dice. You could state a contrary position on a strategy or project at work, or break off a demoralizing relationship even at the risk of loneliness, or start that new little business on the side. Your "dice"?

1. _____
2. _____
3. _____

No one else is going to take chances for you. If you don't do it, you can expect little satisfying change in your life – and very little passion.

Use the Safe

Athletes who are admired and loaded with endorsement deals are photographed using drugs at a party. A CEO in a failing business in a tottering economy spends $1.2 million to redecorate his office. To make a quick dollar, businesses partner with unethical organizations that steal their intellectual property.

> "DARING IDEAS ARE LIKE CHESSMEN MOVED FORWARD; THEY MAY BE BEATEN, BUT THEY MAY START A WINNING GAME."
>
> JOHANN WOLFGANG VON GOETHE, AUTHOR

You have to know when to go into lock-down mode. There are some things just not worth risking. Why put your core business at risk to branch into unknown territory with uncertain payoffs? Why bring in that new employee with a checkered history because he seems smart or interviews well? Why make promises you don't have to make?

But you have to know what to lock up and what to keep out on the table. We all have things we like to secure *tightly* in our grasp. Some writers, for example, hate being edited and fight against it until they are able to ensure the publication of a regrettable manuscript. What do you tend to lock down that would best be kept in the improving reach of others?

1. _____
2. _____
3. _____

And now, what should go into the safe? What needs to be locked up? For some of us, it's our time that needs to be blocked out here and there and fenced off from others. It could be a percentage of income going into savings, whether in our organization or personal lives. It could be an idea that needs to be incubated lest it be crushed in infancy. Yours?

1. _____
2. _____
3. _____

Life can be lived in one of two directions. Either it's theirs unless you take some of it back, or it's yours until you give some of it away. Try to keep the big things locked up until you're sure it's time to share.

And then, if you were wrong or premature in sharing, take it back and lock it up.

Be a Buttoned-Up Gambler

We'll keep our passion at a high level if we learn to be *cautious risk-takers*.

This paradox is about risk-taking and risk-management. Neither one is always bad, and neither one is always good. People who only *take* risks end up broke or dead. People who only *manage* risks end up broke or bored. The key is knowing when to take risk and knowing when to manage it – and more.

We should take a risk when the reward is great *and we know how to minimize the risk*. Taking a risk (even one with great potential reward) if we don't know the downside doesn't make us risk-takers – it makes us fools. All risks should be assessed with a cold, calculating eye on the potential for harm, and the likelihood that this harm is going to occur.

We should avoid a risk when the reward is unclear (no matter how big it seems) or the risk is ambiguous or undefinable – or both. Managing this paradox requires us to be cautious when rewards or risks are unclear and to be gamblers when they're not.

We should be cautious on some things, like cash flow, so we can be gamblers on others, like investing in a new product or making an acquisition. And we should be gamblers on some things, like being the first out with a new idea and capturing market share, so we can have the resources to manage our ongoing business in a cautious, conservative way.

Take a risk sometimes.

> "ENJOY PRESENT PLEASURES IN SUCH A WAY AS NOT TO INJURE FUTURE ONES."
> **SENECA, ROMAN STATESMAN**

TAKE FRESH ACTIONS TO LIVE THIS PARADOX

Describe a risk-taker you know. What do you like about his or her gambling that you could adopt?

_____
_____
_____

Describe a risk-minimizer you know. What do you like about his or her caution that you could adopt?

_____
_____
_____

Where could more caution in one area of your personal or work life give you more opportunity to take risks in some other area?

_____
_____
_____

Where could more risk-taking in one area of your personal or work life give you more resources to live in a freer or more independent way in some other area?

_____
_____
_____

If you know what not to risk, risk-taking is a beautiful thing.

PARADOX 4: BE A RACEHORSE AND A PLOW HORSE

FIVE PARADOXES FOR PRODUCING BETTER PERFORMANCE
Be a Rock and a Stream
Eliminate Distractions and Listen for Input
Throw the Dice and Use the Safe
> **BE A RACEHORSE AND A PLOW HORSE**
Push Hard and Cut Way Back

Be a Racehorse

Getting "stuck" is a very human situation.

There we are, going over the same ground again and again. Didn't we just deal with that issue last year? How did we hire the same kind of person? Why are we discussing this issue for the twenty-third time?

Passion is ablaze when you run fast, blinders on, not looking around you or behind you. Just see the goal and run for it as fast as you can. It's moving past "first things first" to "first things *only*." It's refusing to let yourself be sidetracked. Think about a time when you ran fast and straight. What happened? What did that look like?

_____

_____

_____

What lessons can you take away from that experience? What can you learn so that you can run fast in other areas in the future?

1. _____
2. _____
3. _____

If you get what you expect (and that principle works in a good part of life), you'll get much more that you want to keep if you expect to win.

Be a Plow Horse

For a racehorse, the gold comes from flying over the ground. For a plow horse, the gold comes from digging up the ground. Sometimes the goal is out there and you have to run like crazy to get it. And other times, the goal is right there under your feet.

> "LIFE DOESN'T GIVE YOU ALL THE PRACTICE RACES YOU NEED."
>
> JESSE OWENS, OLYMPIC RUNNER

George Washington Carver adopted the commitment of a plow horse when it came to a little item called the "peanut." Everyone else saw an inconsequential plant. Carver saw potential. He worked and worked until he found scores of uses for the lowly peanut.

But to be an effective plow horse, you have to know where not to dig. Some ground is just too hard, and even after you've broken your back on it you still have nothing. We all have problems or issues or even opportunities that drive us to dig down deep into the details, but we can sense that it's barren ground. Where is your barren ground? Where have you dug down and gotten nothing to show for your inch-by-inch labor in the sweltering heat? And what can you do to throw off the harness?

_____

_____

_____

Being a plow horse requires us to do some hard work, with the potential return – the harvest – way down the road. That makes it easy to procrastinate. What's an area that you know will pay off with a large crop if you can make yourself start plowing? And what will you do to start moving on that area *now*?

_____

_____

_____

Be an Industrious Sprinter

Deeper passion is waiting for us if we practice the best of both, if we find our way to being *muscular thoroughbreds*.

You start with running. It's too easy in life to get bogged down. We can dwell on a decision or course of action far longer than it's worth, and let it keep us from finding better ground. You can think, "I've already invested time in this [degree program, career, relationship, association, church], so even though it doesn't seem to be working, it seems prudent to keep going." Or, "I don't want to move on until I've explored every possible bit of potential here." Or, "They promised they'd [support me, buy from me, endorse me, stick with me], so I'm going to keep meeting with them and expecting them to deliver."

> **"THE WAGON RESTS IN WINTER, THE SLEIGH IN SUMMER, THE HORSE NEVER."** PROVERB

Get over it. Use your instincts. Follow your passions. When it becomes fairly obvious that something is a dead end, turn around. Cover more ground. See what's out there. You don't want to spend your life pawing around on a hardscrabble piece of ground when there's rich bottomland a few miles down the road.

And when you find that rich land, stop running and start plowing. Put the bugle away. Stop timing yourself. Go deep, plant much, work the ground, make it your own.

You want to know when to fly over the ground and when to dig it up. You have to run: you can't dig up all of the ground or you'll never cover what is yours, never cross the finish line. And you have to dig: you can't just run or you'll never notice what you're missing, never find the gold.

You want to run fast so you can find the land worth plowing. And you want to plow up the rich ground so you won't spend your life chasing the next thing.

TAKE FRESH ACTIONS TO LIVE THIS PARADOX

Describe a "racehorse" you know. Where could he or she get a big return by slowing down and digging?

_____
_____
_____

Describe a "plow horse" you know. Where could he or she get a big return by giving up the digging and running instead?

_____
_____
_____

Where do you need to slow yourself down and start digging?

_____
_____
_____

Where do you need to stop digging and start running fast?

_____
_____
_____

We've been told to "never look back" and also to "make hay while the sun shines." A passionate managing of this paradox leads you to do both. Running and plowing, speed and thoroughness – it's all part of a full life.

PARADOX 5: PUSH HARD AND CUT WAY BACK

FIVE PARADOXES FOR PRODUCING BETTER PERFORMANCE
Be a Rock and a Stream
Eliminate Distractions and Listen for Input
Throw the Dice and Use the Safe
Be a Racehorse and a Plow Horse
> **PUSH HARD AND CUT WAY BACK**

Push Hard

Two of Andrew Carnegie's three keys to success: "industry" and "persistence." We might call them hard work and intensity.

Unless you're ready to rely on dumb luck, there are simply no shortcuts to passionate success. You don't become an accomplished *anything* – writer, speaker, teacher, scientist, engineer, doctor, lawyer, chef, mentor, athlete – without a lot of hard work and unrelenting intensity.

If anything is worth doing, it's worth pushing ourselves hard to do it. Here's a bit of news: *There really is no such thing as "working too hard."* We can, however:

- Fail to put necessary boundaries around work – nutrition, exercise, sleep, time for relationships and relaxation – and confuse "working too much" with "working too hard."
- Do work that kills our souls, and discover that working at *anything* that stirs no passion, or that uses only a fraction of our talent, is *always* "too hard."
- Work at a place that is noxious or with people who are obnoxious, which can make *showing up* seem "too hard."

Describe where you might be "working too much," or "working too boring," or "working too toxic":

_____

_____

_____

Where do you need to push yourself harder? Where could more intensity bring you more success?

_____

_____

"HARD WORK IS A PRISON SENTENCE ONLY IF IT DOES NOT HAVE MEANING. ONCE IT DOES, IT BECOMES THE KIND OF THING THAT MAKES YOU GRAB YOUR WIFE AROUND THE WAIST AND DANCE A JIG."

MALCOLM GLADWELL, AUTHOR[39]

Cut Way Back

We can work really hard and never really enjoy it. We've done a lot today, the schedule was full, we never had a minute to ourselves – but wait, what did it matter? Did any of it really count? Did we make even the slightest difference? If the cruise ship never pulls into port, all we see is ocean. Cutting way back can make the times we don't cut back even more productive.

Work is enjoyed most in two places: when we're lost in really valuable work about which we're passionate, and in the "spaces" where we have time to reflect on our work, enjoy our accomplishment, and reap the fruit of our hard labor.

We don't have to cut back only to take multi-week vacations or sabbaticals between jobs. We can cut back by making one day a week or month a "regroup" or "creative" day, where we're still thinking about our work but at a higher, less detailed level (I, Jim, try to do this on Fridays). We can take a break when we've finished a tough task and take ourselves out to lunch. We can take a "dark chocolate" break, or pause to call a friend, or go for a walk. What are some ways, and where are some places, that you can cut way back during your actual work day?

1. _____
2. _____
3. _____

And where could you cut way back at work so you can enjoy more non-work things?

1. _____
2. _____
3. _____

There's always more you can do. The good news is, there's always more you can cut out too.

Be a Person with Intense Zen

We can maximize our whole-life passion by managing this paradox and becoming *zealously serene*.

> "TAKE REST; A FIELD THAT HAS RESTED GIVES A BOUNTIFUL CROP."
> OVID, ROMAN POET

Any life that's either all hard or all easy is a life that's not reaching its potential and is not going to be passionate. We need a dance between the two, a rhythm, a flow from one to the other. This is a concept I (Jim) call *whole-life symmetry*™.[40] Not "work-life balance," as though work and life are opposites, but *symmetry* – all things in proportion, all things at the right time, all things in the best place.

You cut back on some things – the peripheral things, the demanding things – so you can push yourself harder where that effort can really make a difference. You don't cut back in order to avoid doing anything; you cut back so you can do what's really important with even *more* energy and passion and intensity. You cut back so you can create margin, so you have the space to think and create and take on opportunities with fresh insight.

And you push yourself hard so that cutting back isn't a doorway to retirement from life and a path to early death. You don't let the siren song of "take it easy" derail your passion or your life. You push yourself hard enough that you make the cutback times even more enjoyable, more treasured, more memorable.

Managing this paradox means we learn what advances our goals and what cripples us. We accept the pressure that fuels our passion, and we reject the pressure that crushes it.

TAKE FRESH ACTIONS TO LIVE THIS PARADOX

Think of something you're doing at work. Where's the core? What's the most important thing (or things) for you to be working on? What can you cut out on this project or assignment so you can focus on this core?

_____

_____

_____

Where at work could cutting back reinvigorate you? Where could you drop out of just one or two small things that would give you a fresh lease on your work and let you come at it with passion again?

_____

_____

_____

As my friends in Boston might say, "Work wicked hahd." And also, "Play wicked hahd." And tackle it all, the working hard and the playing hard, the times of intensity and the times of margin, the seasons of adding more and the seasons of cutting back, with relentless, margin-filled passion.

Getting Warmer: An Entrepreneur Finds His Way

Gerald Barnes was in Asia when he received a call. He was a vice president of one of the largest clothing retailing corporations in the United States, a position that offered power and wealth. The vice chairman of the corporation wanted him to go to Europe for a meeting.

When Barnes returned from that meeting, Matthew, his son, was crawling.

"It hit me like a ton of bricks," he says. "Am I living to work or am I working to live? I had my priorities out of balance." He made a decision: "I would get out of that very heavy work-hour situation—not right away, but when the opportunity presented itself."

The opportunity came in the form of a position managing 6 major accounts for a wholesale company. Barnes went from working 70 hours a week to working 15 hours a week, earning double to triple his former salary.

"You could only call each account 2 or 3 times a week," he explains. "It didn't take long, but you had to motivate yourself." The position earned straight commission.

In a change in top management, the company ended up with a senior leader who was capable but also had a severe drug addiction and engaged in problematic drug-seeking behaviors. Finally, Barnes could no longer tolerate what felt like "guilt by association."

He began thinking about a colleague in another wholesale apparel company who was in charge of design and production. Between the two of them, he realized, they had all the skills required to run a wholesale clothing company of their own. They quit their jobs and invested $20,000 each to start Michael Gerald, Ltd., hoping to build a $5 million company that would spin off $500,000 a year for each of them and leave them with plenty of time for their families.

"It wasn't done for the money," Barnes says. "It was done for getting my life back."

But the returns surpassed their expectations. The company made $5 million in its third year and went from $5 million to $15 million the next year. Profits more than doubled again the following year, and by the sixth year, they hit $48 million.

"It's not just about the money," Barnes explains. "It's about things you can do with that money, not just for yourself or your family but to help different people or different causes. You want to give something back."

The money also allowed Barnes to pursue other interests—he owns several profitable Ferrari-Maserati dealerships that provide an outlet for his fascination with the cars—and to buy a home on Maui where he can retreat with his family.

Barnes sees passion and skill as fundamental to this kind of business success. "I have a passion for business in general. I want to do whatever I do well. I love to be part of something that's new," he says. "I think if you work hard and you're good at what you do and you're in the right place at the right time, opportunities will present themselves."

Paradoxically, finding those opportunities sometimes requires doing work you don't love for a while until you can do work you love, Barnes argues. "I believe that we have an obligation to do the best job possible with whatever is put in front of us. You may decide down the road that that's not the path you want to pursue, but I've always found that if I applied myself and did the best possible job, given it my best shot even if I didn't like it, opportunities arose. Opportunities that I never even envisioned came out of situations that were not the best."

Opportunities can also come fraught with paradox: should you take risk, or should you avoid it?

"I'm blessed with an entrepreneurial spirit, and I'm a risk taker," says Barnes. "A lot of people will agonize over risk, and when they do make a mistake, they let that affect them for the rest of their lives. They'll never again take a risk. If you're right 7 or 8 out of 10 times, you're going to be tremendously successful. You have to be willing to take that risk and live with the consequences."

He sums up the entrepreneurial life with yet another paradox: "It's very tough, but in that challenge there's tremendous opportunity."

"AT THE HEART OF [TRACK COACH] TEMPLE'S SPRINTING PHILOSOPHY WAS THE SEEMINGLY CONTRADICTORY YET COMMONSENSICAL CONCEPT OF TRAINING HARD TO RUN EASY." DAVID MARANISS, ROME 1960[41]

PLACES WHERE "EITHER" IS THE RIGHT ANSWER

There are areas of life where we can't choose "both" over "either" because there is no "either."

SOME THINGS ARE MUTUALLY EXCLUSIVE. YOU CAN HAVE "A" OR YOU CAN HAVE "B," BUT TRYING TO HAVE BOTH MAKES YOU A VERY CONFUSED PERSON, IF NOT A HYPOCRITE OR A LUNATIC. HERE ARE SOME DEFINITE "EITHERS":

- *Ethics and Values.* You can't be just a little bit honest. You either have integrity or you don't. We can argue about the degree of dishonesty – do we cheat a little or a lot, stretch the truth or break it, mostly live by principles or only when convenient – but ethics are a light switch, either on or off.[*]

- *Vision, Mission, and Strategy.* We either have them or we don't. We either know where we're going and how to get there, or we don't. We can try to substitute strategy for vision or mission, or tactics for strategy, but that doesn't give us a vision or mission or strategy. For more on developing a Vision, Mission, Values, and Behaviors (*VMVB*™) charter, see **The Passion Principle: Designing a Passionate Organization**, the first title in the Passionate Lives and Leaders series.

- *Promises.* We either follow through on our promises or we don't. If we say we're going to do something and then we don't do it, we didn't "almost" keep our promise. We didn't keep it. We broke it. If you find yourself making promises without any intention of keeping them, or wording them to give yourself "wiggle room," see "Ethics and Values" above.

- *Deadlines and Budgets.* In real life we can't "almost" make a deadline, or make it if we're only late by so much. We either make a deadline or we don't. We're either punctual or we're not. We either live within our budgets or we don't. Sometimes there are reasons for missing deadlines and budgets, and there are always excuses, but none of them mean that we made those deadlines or met those budgets.

---

[*] *To learn 10 key ethical principles for 21st-century leaders, see my book* High-Performance Ethics.

- **People Decisions.** We either hire the person or not, promote them or not, terminate them or not. There's no way to avoid the consequences, good or bad. Once the decision is made, there's no "or" about it.

- **Partnerships.** Whatever form a partnership takes, it comes with all of the potential pluses and minuses of a marriage – including its permanency, in memory and consequence if not in contract. We can't "sort of" have a partner or "kind of" be in a partnership and still be completely independent. We're either in the partnership or we're not.

- **Retirement.** We can move on to other activities, but once we've formally retired from a job or position, we're done. The power and prestige and influence and working relationships are all gone.

> "WHEN THERE ARE CLEARLY UNDERSTOOD VISION, MISSION, VALUES, AND BEHAVIORS, THE TENSION OF OPPOSING IDEAS BECOMES AN ACCEPTED CREATIVE FORCE, AS OPPOSED TO A DIVIDING LINE BETWEEN FACTIONS."
>
> KURT MCCASLIN, PRESIDENT & GENERAL MANAGER, ANADARKO (BRAZIL)

Dealing With "Either"

What does this mean? We have to be very careful on these "either only" issues. Once we've made a decision or crossed a line, we're committed. We can always look for a better way to manage paradoxes, including the 15 in this book. But even though we can learn from bad "either" decisions, we can't undo them.

Where are you facing a key "either" situation (see the above "eithers")? And what will you do to make sure you don't choose hastily or incorrectly?

___

Do you see any other "either" categories? Where else in your work or personal life do you see a key "either only" situation?

MERGING COMPETING IDEAS – CLEARING THE OBSTACLES

Throughout this book, we've touched on some of the roadblocks that can keep us from merging the paradoxes in our lives.

LET'S TAKE A LOOK AT SOME OTHER OBSTACLES, SO WE CAN MASTER PARADOXES AND BUILD LIVES THAT PASSIONATELY CONTRIBUTE TO THE LIVES AROUND US.

Obstacle 1: False Pride

We've heard people say things that confirm they're locked in exclusively on one side or the other of a paradox, and darn proud of it. "I'm an optimist" or "I'm a realist." "I'm a creative person" or "I'm a disciplined person." "I'm a tough-minded manager" or "I'm a people person." "I like to take a risk" or "I like to play it safe."

Sometimes, these positions have become big parts of who we are, and this rigidity can make it very hard to *look* at the other side of paradoxes, much less adopt them. This is really bad pride – pride that we're half-baked.

Obstacle 2: No Experience

The world is full of paradoxes and full of ways to avoid facing them. If we're like most people, we've never had any training in managing paradoxes and not much practice in living them.

But now, you have the tool for managing these paradoxes. Live inside these ideas for just a few weeks, and you'll have more experience with paradoxes than most government leaders or CEOs.

Obstacle 3: Leaders or Organizations that Demand "Either"

We've worked with thousands of leaders in hundreds of organizations, and we can say that many of them are happily situated on one side or the other of a paradox. There are organizations that analyze the past not just to paralysis but to death, and other organizations that ignore the past and keep repeating its disasters. There are top-down, micromanaging, autocratic organizations and input-seeking, empowering, consensus-is-god organizations. There are places primed above all to take even unnecessary risk, and others immersed in crippling consistency.

The leader who says, "You're either with me or you're not," has created a false dichotomy that avoids the nuanced position, "I'm with you, boss, but not on this point."

Obstacle 4: Mental Laziness

Mental laziness is certainly a barrier to living the *Paradox Principle*™. It's almost always easier in the short run to pick one side or the other of a paradox. But only in the short run. The long-term consequences of ignoring the other side are *always harder and almost always bad*.

We've given you lots of places in this book to develop an ease with paradoxes. We hope you use them. It will get easier and easier to think and act this way, and you will separate yourself from your colleagues in a distinctive and significant way.

Obstacle 5: Relationships that Divide the Paradox

In marriage and parenting, it's not uncommon to find one parent who is "soft" and the other "hard," one who is a "good-time Charlie" and the other a drill sergeant, one who likes to spend and the other who likes to save, one who wants to socialize and one who wants to hole up in the castle. This approach can sort of work for a bit, but it mostly creates room for anger and arguments, and for children to play fast and loose in the gaps and take advantage of the "two-person divide."

The same is true in organizations. Someone can think, "I'm a realistic, no baloney, take-no-prisoners leader, but my right-hand person takes care of the motivation and teamwork and people stuff." This thinking is an illusion. It can work, if by *work* we mean "produce some results." But this division of labor will never work as well as both people finding a way to live these 15 paradoxes.

Obstacle 6: Confusing Paradoxes with "Tradeoffs"

There are many areas of life where there are tradeoffs. If we have X dollars to spend, we can spend them on this or on that, but we can't spend them on both. Tradeoffs are different from paradoxes (where we want more of both sides), and they're different from a true "either" (where we can only have one side). With a tradeoff, we can't have more of both. The more we have of one, the less we'll have of the other. But we can have some of both: we can split X dollars in many different ways between this and that.

The problem comes when we think of a paradox as a tradeoff: If I'm more disciplined, that will kill my creativity. If I celebrate mistakes, that will demolish excellence. If I change my mind, that will tell people I'm weak. One of the glories of a paradox is that we can have more of both and then some. When we treat paradoxes as tradeoffs, we're likely to end up with less of each one.

RATE YOUR ORGANIZATION

On a scale of 1 to 10, rate your organization on each of these obstacles. A rating of **1** means there is no evidence of this obstacle in your organization, and **10** means your organization is in danger of being brought to a halt in managing paradoxes effectively.

False Pride	1	2	3	4	5	6	7	8	9	10
No Experience	1	2	3	4	5	6	7	8	9	10
Demanding "Either"	1	2	3	4	5	6	7	8	9	10
Mental Laziness	1	2	3	4	5	6	7	8	9	10
Dividing the Paradox	1	2	3	4	5	6	7	8	9	10
Confusing Paradoxes with Tradeoffs	1	2	3	4	5	6	7	8	9	10

Now, jot down why you assigned each score and what could be done to improve it.

False Pride _____

No Experience _____

Demanding "Either" _____

Mental Laziness _____

Dividing the Paradox _____

Confusing Paradoxes with Tradeoffs _____

A Life in Paradox

"Never did I imagine in my young days that my life would be focused on religion and diplomacy and the UN," says Bawa Jain, the Secretary General for the World Council of Religious Leaders of the United Nations.

A businessman by training, Jain left India for the United States at the urging of his religious mentor. *"He quite simply said, 'Start work at the UN,'"* Jain recalls. *"I didn't know what that meant, but my mentor, my guru as we say in India, said so. Since then, I've been focusing my energies into bringing religion to the work of the United Nations. In the year 2000, we had the Millennium Summit, a gathering of over 1200 religious leaders from 120 countries. And for the first time, they assembled in the General Assembly Hall of the United Nations."*

The work of the summit didn't concern promoting the spread of religion. *"We didn't discuss theology or philosophy,"* says Jain. *"Rather, we wanted to see what individually and collectively each religious leader can do to bring peace to the world. Peace is not just the absence of war. Peace means dealing with social challenges that we are confronted with. That's where the UN becomes important. My own experience was that because it was the UN, people from every religion came. It was a neutral platform. And this is a platform at the highest level of the political structure of the world. Our goal is to see how we can harness religious resources to work for a global goal."*

To hear Jain describe it, accomplishing a goal of this magnitude is an exercise in paradox management.

"If we have to build an integrated framework for peace, the 3 important sectors are business, politics, and religion. Politicians, to be elected, need to be supported by the masses. Who has the support of and access to the masses? Religious leaders. And who benefits from a stable, viable, peaceful environment? Business. We need these 3 spheres to work rather closely. If you look at history, sometimes they have not worked together. Rather, they are blaming each other. We must bring them to the table together to meet on global issues, so they see the real value religion can contribute, rather than religion being demonized and abused as a source of conflict and violence in the world. This was one of the commitments of the Millennium Summit: to disavow all violence in the name of religion. So, religious leaders have to have the courage to stand up and say, 'Not in the name of religion.' We try to provide resources to do that wherever there's a conflict."

In one recent example, Jewish leaders sought out Muslim and Hindu leaders after the attacks in Mumbai. The leaders committed to finding ways to discuss differences rather than falling *back on violence.*

"For me, any religious leader fundamentally is a bridge," says Jain. "How can we bring about enough of these young leaders to believe that they are a bridge, to believe that the work of God is to be a bridge, and to actually go into the community and be a bridge?"

Jain recommends the harmony that comes from embracing paradox as a way of life. For him, people need to order their internal lives even as they reach out to others.

"What is the value of your life? What are you doing with your life? That is more important than what you are acquiring materially. You go and share the work of God with others and bring about a change in their lives, even in a small way. That's what life's purpose should be, ultimately. But if you seek to do all the wonderful work in the world and your inner state is in shambles, you cannot do the work. It just doesn't make sense."

Jain holds himself to a simple but challenging standard for evaluating his own life.

"The yardstick for that is, if I were to fall down today and die, what is it that I want people to remember me for? Then I reflect and see, am I happy with that? If not, then I keep working towards what it is that I want people to remember me for. That's what drives me."
Belief or analysis? Faith or science? Trust or logic?

Of course.

TIME FOR ACTION

In a very short space, we have covered a lot of ground. You might be tempted to try to master all of these paradoxes right away, but don't give in to that temptation.

We suggest that you take on one of these paradoxes each week for the next 15 weeks. If you take more than a week per paradox, you won't be moving at a fast enough clip. If you take less than a week per paradox, you probably won't introduce much meaningful change.

So put one in your calendar for each week, leaving out any weeks where you are fully scheduled with high-priority work or are on vacation. In 6 months or so, you will have mastered these personal paradoxes, a wonderful source of personal advantage that very few leaders – no matter how brilliant – have even *thought* about effectively.

For more on building an organization that thinks better collectively than its individual members can think alone, see **The Thinking Principle: Using Passion to Innovate and Create Value,** the third title in the Passionate Lives & Leaders series.

FAQ

In this book, have you covered all of the paradoxes a leader can face?

No. Leadership and organizational cultures are loaded with paradoxes. We've covered 15 of the most common and important personal paradoxes that leaders face. Jim has written another book, *Broaden the Vision and Narrow the Focus: Managing in a World of Paradox*, which covers 20 organizational paradoxes. He breaks these paradoxes into 4 areas – leadership, culture, talent, strategy – with 5 paradoxes in each area. Don't miss it.

Really, how common are paradoxes?

Competing ideas are everywhere. We've given you 15 in this book, and 20 more in the book *Broaden the Vision and Narrow the Focus: Managing in a World of Paradox*. And although these 35 are some of the most critical, they by no means exhaust the list.

What happens if we don't adopt the Paradox Principle™?

Most leaders have developed a leadership style that only incorporates one side of these two-sided gems. When their normal approach stops working, they swing to the opposite approach. As a result, organizations end up on the "pendulum": back and forth—here immersed in the present and there swamped by the future, here controlling and dictating and there involving and sharing power, now striving for consistency but then driving for change. No one is able to develop any proficiency with either approach because the visits to each side are so brief.

If this paradox business is so important, why aren't more people writing about it?

Frankly, it's a lot easier to write simplistic stuff, and it's usually easier to sell it. But eventually, most leaders come to a frustrating realization: the "experts" are giving advice that just doesn't seem consistent. Benchmark your competitors, or find a unique value proposition? Motivate the troops to get them fired up or tell the troops the ugly truth? Focus on quarterly earnings or focus on long-term growth? There are books on each side; none of them complete.

How can we know when something is a paradox?

Leaders deal with conflicting ideas every day. Some of these ideas are tradeoffs. Some are downright contradictions. But world-class leaders know how to recognize the competing ideas that can be merged—and how to turn those mergers into a source of competitive advantage. It starts by taking the time to immerse yourself in the 15 paradoxes in this book. The process will change the way you think. You'll be able to see false "either only" ideas (false contradictions) and false tradeoffs quickly – and eventually, easily. It isn't a matter of memorizing a list of paradoxes; it's a matter of learning how to *think paradoxically.*

How can I avoid living in only one side of a paradox?

It comes down to choice. Once you see the paradox – and you should be pretty good at that if you've gone through this book – it comes down to making a decision and having the willpower to force yourself out of old ways of thinking and acting. Most leaders and organizations are biased to implement one competing idea or the other—and they miss out on the returns that come from acting on *both.* But you can learn how to be a world-class leader who merges competing ideas to produce top-tier results. Your world will be different - and much richer.

For more on this powerful subject of paradox, please see James Lucas's full-length book **Broaden the Vision and Narrow the Focus:** *Managing in a World of Paradox.*

Luman International also has an in-depth assessment, the Thinking Quotient™, which will provide you tremendous insight into your organization's Thinking DNA, Infrastructure, Leadership, People, and Transformation/Adaptive Capacity.

We offer a full-day course, "Leading Mergers of Competing Ideas," and a number of keynotes or short presentations on the topic, including "Think: How World-Class Leaders Merge Competing Ideas™."

We can assist you on several aspects of designing and building a thinking organization with our Signature Processes, including "Developing Paradox-Based Leadership™" and "Implementing the PitStop Protocol."

For more information, please visit lumaninternational.com.

"MANAGING THROUGH PARADOX IS BOTH FUNDAMENTAL AND PROVOCATIVE. LUCAS SHOWS US HOW EFFECTIVE ORGANIZATIONS BEHAVE IN FLEXIBLE YET SOMETIMES CONTRADICTORY WAYS, AND HE PROVIDES LEADERS WITH...STEPS TO IMPROVE BUSINESS DECISIONS AND MASTER THE *PARADOX PRINCIPLE*™."

ROBERT BARRETT, PRESIDENT & CEO,
INCHARGE INSTITUTE OF AMERICA

Endnotes

1. *As quoted by Lance Morrow, "Kennedy's Secret Pain."* Time *11 May 2003.*

2. *Stengel, Richard. "Mandela: His 8 Lessons of Leadership."* Time *21 July 2008: 48.*

3. *Welch, Jack.* Winning: The Ultimate Business How-To Book. *New York :HarperCollins, 2005.*

4. *Bohr, Niels.* Essays 1958-1962 on Atomic Physics and Human Knowledge. *Woodbridge: Ox Bow Press, 1987.*

5. *As quoted by Dr. Robert Hemenway, University of Kansas Chancellor, in his commencement address, May 2004.*

6. *Accessed 14 September 2008. Available: http://www.quoteworld.org/quotes/4650.*

7. *Accessed 23 September 2008. Available: http://www.famousquotesandauthors.com/authors/john_heywood_quotes.html.*

8. *Accessed 27 September 2008. Available: http://quotationsbook.com/quote/22888/.*

9. *Accessed 12 September 2008. Available: http://www.giga-usa.com/quotes/authors/robert_townsend_a001.htm.*

10. *This is the number given by Malcolm Gladwell in his book* Outliers: The Story of Success. *New York: Little, Brown and Company, 2008.*

11. *Accessed 24 September 2008. Available: http://www.saidwhat.co.uk/quotes/political/winston_churchill.*

12. *Jefferson, Thomas.* The Political Writings of Thomas Jefferson. *Ed. Merrill D. Peterson. Charlottesville: Thomas Jefferson Foundation, 1993.*

13. *Plato and Benjamin Jowett.* Euthyphro, Apology, Crito, Phaedo. *Amherst: Prometheus Books, 1988.*

14. *Johnson, Paul.* The Renaissance: A Short History. *New York: Random House, 2002: 147.*

15. *Accessed: 3 October 2008. Available: http://www.goodreads.com/quotes/show/32118.*

16. *Accessed 4 October 2008. Available: http://www.collegiateentrepreneur.com/focus.html.*

17. *Johnson, Paul.* The Renaissance: A Short History. *New York: Random House, 2002: 147.*

18. *See my book* Broaden the Vision and Narrow the Focus *– the chapter by the same name. First we broaden our horizons, and then we get down to the areas of greatest interest and impact.*

19. *Kluger, Jeffrey.* Simplexity. *New York: Hyperion, 2008.*

20. *Accessed 14 October 2008. Available: http://www.wow4u.com/andrewcarnegie/index.html.*

21. *Accessed 14 October 2008. Available: http://www.quoteblock.com/quote/time-is-the-scarcest-resource-and-unless-it-is/.*

22. *If you want to know more about this business application, see the chapter in* Broaden the Vision and Narrow the Focus *titled "Reduce Costs and Increase Spending."*

23. *Accessed 14 November 2008. Available: http://www.dailycelebrations.com/092100.htm*

24. *Accessed 17 September 2008. Available: http://cervantes.thefreelibrary.com/.*

25. *Accessed: 12 October 2008. Available: http://www.quotationspage.com/quote/31023.html.*

26. *To learn more about PitStops™ in a business context, contact Luman International.*

27. *Accessed 2 September 2008. Available: http://www.brainyquote.com/quotes/authors/l/leo_tolstoy.html.*

[28] *Accessed 3 December 2008. Available: http://www.brainyquote.com/quotes/authors/t/tommy_lasorda.html.*

[29] *Lombardi, Jr., Vince.* What It Takes to Be #1. *New York: McGraw-Hill, 2001.*

[30] *Accessed 2 November 2008. Available: http://www.coachk.com/quotes.php.*

[31] *Accessed 3 September 2008. Available: http://quotations.about.com/cs/inspirationquotes/a/Leadership15.htm.*

[32] *Accessed 4 October 2008. Available: http://quotations.about.com/cs/inspirationquotes/a/Leadership18.htm.*

[33] *Goethals, George R., and James MacGregor Burns.* Encyclopedia of Leadership. *Thousand Oaks: Sage, 2004.*

[34] *Accessed 2 October 2008. Available: http://www.famousquotesandauthors.com/topics/principle_quotes.html.*

[35] *Goethals, George R., and James MacGregor Burns.* Encyclopedia of Leadership. *Thousand Oaks: Sage, 2004.*

[36] *Accessed 14 September 2008. Available: http://www.google.com/search?sourceid=navclient&ie=UTF-8&rlz=1T4DKUS_enUS312&q=lao+tzu.*

[37] *Quoted in "Thoughts on the Business Life."* Forbes *8 November 1982: 280.*

[38] *Alda, Alan.* Never Have Your Dog Stuffed. *New York: Random House, 2006.*

[39] *Gladwell, Malcolm.* Outliers: The Story of Success. *New York: Little, Brown and Company, 2008: 150.*

[40] *See my book* High-Performance Ethics, *the chapter titled "Find Symmetry."*

[41] *Maraniss, David.* Rome 1960. *New York: Simon & Schuster, 2008.*

JAMES R. LUCAS

James R. Lucas is a recognized authority on leadership and cultural design. He is a groundbreaking author and thought leader, provocative speaker, and experienced consultant on these crucial topics.

Jim is President and CEO of Luman International, an organization which he founded in 1983. This firm is dedicated to Developing Passionate, Thinking, Pure-Performance Organizations™ and their leaders, people, and teams.

Clients are from sectors as diverse as health care, pharmaceuticals, medical devices, financial services, accounting, energy, chemicals, forest and paper products, transportation, computer hardware, diversified manufacturing, consumer products, diversified business services, construction, state government, and federal government. They range from Fortune 1000 public companies and private for-profit organizations to not-for-profits and government agencies.

Jim has written numerous curricula for business and leadership seminars, as well as many essays and articles. In addition to the PASSIONATE LIVES AND LEADERS series, he is the author of five other landmark books on leadership and organizational development:

- High-Performance Ethics: *10 Timeless Principles for Next Generation Leadership*
- Broaden the Vision and Narrow the Focus: *Managing in a World of Paradox*
- The Passionate Organization: *Igniting the Fire of Employee Commitment*
- Balance of Power: *Fueling Employee Power without Relinquishing Your Own*
- Fatal Illusions: *Shredding a Dozen Unrealities That Can Keep Your Organization from Success*

Prior to founding Luman International, Jim was President of EMCI, a high-tech design and manufacturer of aerospace systems and medical devices. Before that, he held managerial and executive positions at Hallmark Cards, VF Corporation, and Black & Veatch Consulting Engineers.

Jim is an award-winning senior faculty member of the American Management Association, where he served for several years as a charter member of the Faculty Advisory Council. He taught its premier course, The Course for Presidents (in which he was and is the highest-rated faculty member), and is the overall highest-rated faculty member in the history of the AMA. He is also a frequent presenter at the Center for Leadership & Executive Development. Jim has an extensive speaking schedule, in which he addresses topics from his books and research, and has been interviewed frequently on radio and television.

Jim received his education in leadership, business, economics, and engineering at the University of Missouri (Columbia and Rolla), where he received his Ph.D. (h.c.). He has also taught at Rockhurst University. Jim is past president of the Academy of Engineering Management, a member of the American Society for Training and Development, a member of the American Society of Engineering Management, a senior member of the Society of Manufacturing Engineers, and a registered professional engineer in Missouri and Kansas.

Jim has been honored with continuous listings in *Who's Who in America* (1999-2009), *Who's Who in the World* (1989-2008), and *Who's Who in Finance & Industry* (1989-2009).

PHIL HOTSENPILLER

Phil Hotsenpiller is an executive coach who brings his wealth of professional experience, creativity, and spiritual insight to passionate leaders around the world.

Phil is the founder and President of New York Executive Coaching Group, a firm that has assisted Presidents, CEOs, and other professionals to achieve breakthrough results in their professional and personal lives. His clients are a diverse and accomplished array of leaders in many sectors: arts and entertainment, finance and industry, and religious and not-for-profit.

Phil is also the Executive Director of the not-for-profit International Freedom (IF). IF is working with its partners to build 200 education centers for Dalit children and 200 vocational training centers for Dalit women throughout India. Using the power of documentary film, International Freedom also seeks to raise awareness among Hollywood "influencers" of the plight of the Dalit people in order to bring about lasting change. IF's acclaimed documentary, DELETES, was selected to compete in the Artivist Film Festival and the HollyShorts Film Festival, where it earned the Audience Choice Award. In addition, IF has recruited more than 1000 volunteers to serve urban Los Angeles, feeding the homeless and creating after-school programs and health clinics.

Throughout his career, Phil has worked extensively on issues at the nexus of leadership, artistry, and spirituality. Previously, he served as adjunct professor in a division of Southern Theological Seminary and Union Theological Seminary. He has spoken on leadership and theology throughout Mexico, Brazil, Paraguay, El Salvador, Honduras, Guatemala, Romania, Yugoslavia, and France, working with the European Team of Christian Associates International in the area of leadership development. He was one of 25 selected to serve on the Pastors Task Force for the War on Drugs organized by former U.S. "drug czar" William Bennett. Phil also founded *One Purpose*, a weekly television show on WSFJ-TV and a daily radio broadcast on WRFD radio.

Phil continues to address these issues, facilitating a weekly group of 100 prominent actors and young leaders in the Hollywood entertainment industry. With bestselling graphic novel artist/illustrator Rob Liefeld, Phil is a founding partner of 12 Gates Productions, an entertainment company producing a full line of graphic novels, lithographs, DVDs, feature-length films, and video games. He currently serves as Teaching Pastor at Yorba Linda Friends Church in Southern California; YLFC was recently honored as one of the 100-fastest growing churches in the United States. As a leader of discovery trips to Europe, Phil teaches European history, art, philosophy, religion, and culture in Geneva, Amsterdam, and Aix-en-Provence. These trips provide participants with an understanding of different cultures and build bridges between passionate people around the world.

Phil received his education in history, religion, political science, and English literature at Southwest Baptist University. He earned his Master of Divinity from New Orleans Baptist Theological Seminary and completed postgraduate studies at Christ Church College, Oxford University.

Phil is married to Tammy Hotsenpiller, author of *A Taste of Humanity* (2009) and co-founder and designer of Humanity™ for All, LLC, a cutting-edge clothing line noted for its original art with an urban flair and its strong links with dozens of social justice organizations. Songwriter Tye-V (Nycolia Turman) is writing lyrics for an upcoming Humanity™ album.

The Passionate Lives & Leaders Series

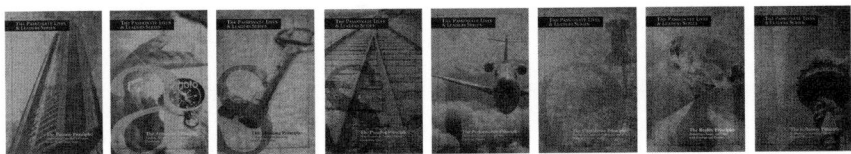

Book 1 - The Passion Principle: *Designing a Passionate Organization*
Book 2 - The Attraction Principle: *Finding, Keeping and Teaming Passionate People*
Book 3 - The Thinking Principle: *Using Passion to Innovate and Create Value*
Book 4 - The Paradox Principle: *How Passionate Leaders Merge Competing Ideas*
Book 5 - The Performance Principle: *Delivering Results through the Power of Passion*
Book 6 - The Confidence Principle: *Discovering Your Life's Passion and a Place to Live It*
Book 7 - The Reality Principle: *Exploiting Change and Crisis with Courage and Passion*
Book 8 - The Influence Principle: *Communicating and Coaching to Ignite Passion*

You and every member of your organization will be inspired by this 8-book series, in which real-world leaders share their experiences in building passionate teams and organizations. Read how the ultimate competitive advantage is harnessing the passion that leads to outstanding performance!

For more about **THE PASSIONATE LIVES AND LEADERS SERIES,** *visit www.livesandleaders.com.*

To order, or to learn more about volume discounts for individual books and sets, visit Quintessential Books at www.quintessentialbooks.com.

To learn more about implementing these principles, visit Luman International at www.lumaninternational.com.

READ BOLDLY. THINK DEEPLY. LIVE PASSIONATELY.
www.quintessentialbooks.com